"Why should not the New Englander be in search of new adventures?"
THOREAU: *Walden*

Country Inns and Back Roads

New England, West Coast, Canada,
Middle Atlantic, South, Midwest, Rocky Mts.

VOLUME XVII

BY THE BERKSHIRE TRAVELLER
Norman T. Simpson

THE BERKSHIRE TRAVELLER PRESS
Stockbridge, Massachusetts

SELECTED TITLES FROM BERKSHIRE TRAVELLER PRESS

Country Inns and Back Roads, North America
Country Inns and Back Roads, Britain and Ireland
Country Inns and Back Roads, Europe
Country Inns and Back Roads Cookbook
Bed & Breakfast, American Style
A Guide to Music Festivals in America
Music Festivals in Europe
Country Bed and Breakfast Places in Canada
Where to Eat in Canada
Inns of Ontario
The Caribbean . . . The Inn Way
Switzerland . . . The Inn Way
How to Open a Country Inn
Europe on 84¢ A Day
Measured Drawings of Shaker Furniture
Adventure Travel

COVER PAINTING   Sheila Granda

Sheila has given us a New England Colonial village near sundown. It is early April, 1775. Perhaps Samuel Adams or John Hancock has just arrived at the inn to enjoy dinner and greet old friends before adjourning to the church, which also served as a meeting house, to speak about Parliament's most recent Intolerable Act. Soon the men of this village will heed the call to arms, and the Great Revolt will be under way. The inn may well have survived 200 years and still be thriving today.

BOOK DESIGN AND DRAWINGS: Janice Lindstrom

Library of Congress 70-615644
ISBN 0-912-94470-6

Printed in the United States of America by The Studley Press Inc., Dalton, Massachusetts
Published by Berkshire Traveller Press, Stockbridge, Massachusetts 01262

PREFACE

Before this book went to press I was browsing through some of the earlier editions, particularly those in the late 1960s and the early 1970s. I enjoyed rereading the accounts of my first visits to many inns that are still included in the book. In those days it was necessary to define what a country inn was. The great value of the book lay in the fact that it told everyone *where* they were. Country inns were just not well known in those days.

Today that is all turned around. There has been a significant proliferation of inns, whether they are full-service, offering both lodgings and all meals, or bed-and-breakfast inns. As a result the governing standards of this book have naturally become highly selective, and only inns of mature experience and proven capabilities have been included.

As I suspected it might, this book has finally reached its optimum dimensions. Even though the scope of the book is North America, the number of inns included will not increase. Inns from a waiting list take the place of inns that are not being continued. This happens most frequently when there is a change in ownership and we must regretfully omit the inn from the following edition. It is reentered only after I pay a visit to the new innkeepers at least a year later.

Almost from the very beginning in 1966 each inn in this book has become a member of an informal innkeeping association through which each is vigorously encouraged to maintain the highest standards. These principles are strengthened by yearly regional innkeeper's meetings throughout North America and a three-day general meeting annually. The association provides a continual interchange of ideas and information among the inns.

In my evaluation of the important qualities that I am delighted to find in an inn, I look for a distinct personal involvement with guests on the part of the innkeepers and their staff; the rudiments of good innkeeping that include clean, comfortable lodging rooms furnished with individuality; an imaginative menu with good, well-prepared food; and an atmosphere that encourages guests to become acquainted with each other. In the decision as to which of the many applicants to include, one of the determining factors is their enthusiasm for holding to the high ideals and standards which the inns themselves have set for the past seventeen years.

Seventeen, or even one-hundred-and-seventeen, years has not seen any changes in the basic fundamentals of good innkeeping, although most of today's innkeepers are families who have sought out innkeeping as a second career. In many cases they have moved their own family heirlooms and personal furniture into the inn and are sharing them with their guests. Each inn is a highly individual enterprise reflecting the philosophies, tastes, and enthusiasms of the innkeeper and his family. That's one of the great reasons why inns continue to grow in popularity each year.

In much the same way that staying at inns is a different experience from staying at commercial, impersonal hotels or motels, so is the attitude of the inn guest different from that of the motel traveler. The ideal inn guest is someone who values the qualities offered by a country inn, and who contributes to that ambience with his or her own consideration and friendliness. When visiting an inn, think of yourself as a guest in the home of a good friend—in the smaller, more intimate inns becoming friends with the innkeeper and his family is a distinct possibility. And there is always the opportunity to make friends with other inn guests.

Here are some basic guidelines for reservations and cancellations in most of the inns listed in this book:

A deposit is required for a confirmed reservation. Guests are requested to please note arrival and departure dates carefully. The deposit will be forfeited if the guest arrives after date specified or departs before final date of reservation. Refund will be made only if cancelled from 7 to 14 days (depending on the policy of the individual inn) in advance of arrival date and a service charge will be deducted from the deposit.

It must be understood that a deposit insures that your accommodations will be available as confirmed, and also assures the inn that the accommodations are sold as confirmed. Therefore, when situations arise necessitating your cancellation less than the allowed number of days in advance, your deposit will not be refunded.

WHAT IS INNKEEPING REALLY LIKE?

Each year I receive many dozens of letters from readers who are considering a second career in country innkeeping. There is a common refrain in each of these letters that has a most familiar ring: "We have visited many of the country inns listed in your book, and we both agree that we would like to get away from the hurly-burly of the city and take up residence in the country where the pace is much slower and more agreeable to us."

These letter-writers usually reveal that on the average they are somewhere between 40 and 45 years old with approximately 2½ children, 8 to 13 years old. They have a certain amount of equity in the mortgage of their suburban home, and with that, plus a family loan, they are able to muster an adequate amount of negotiable cash and securities toward the new venture.

Inquiries are almost always made as to books and also other sources such as government pamphlets (there are none) that might be available on operating inns. Typical questions: Is there a specific way to find out when an inn is for sale, where are the best real estate agents to assist in finding inn property, how much money is needed for a down payment, how much should be kept in escrow against emergencies, how many operating dollars are necessary, what are some of the absolute essentials necessary to go into the country-inn business?

I'm happy to say that the Berkshire Traveller Press recently published a book by Karen Etsell and Elaine Brennan, innkeepers of The Bramble Inn on Cape Cod, entitled *How To Open A Country Inn* which can be ordered directly from us for $8.95 including postage.

Packed with the most detailed advice and information concerning all aspects of opening and running a country inn, *How To Open A Country Inn* also provides interesting and at times amusing reading with anecdotes and incidents that have happened to the authors and other innkeepers, and there are some humorous cartoons by Leo Garel.

Prospective innkeepers will benefit from the careful attention to such issues as investment capital, demographic studies, accounting procedures, purchasing tips (including a detailed shopping list), organization of personnel, running a dining room, advertising and publicity, and expansion and growth, as well as such important points as establishing a personality or focus for the inn, and the need for an atmosphere of true hospitality and warmth.

To provide further insight into the business of innkeeping, once again I have distributed throughout this book comments from various innkeepers. An attempt has been made to keep a balance between the pros and cons of innkeeping and I hope these personal observations will be of value to all those readers who wonder what innkeeping is really like.

WHAT IS INNKEEPING REALLY LIKE?

"Reflecting over six years now, I think the nicest thing about innkeeping is the friendships we've made with our guests. I feel much a part of some of these peoples' lives now. I know their jobs, their children, and how they feel about certain issues. I look forward to seeing them open the front door and hearing of the new things that have happened to them. And it's not just Tom and me. There's little turnover with our staff so that they, too, have come to know our guests. It must be just as comforting for them to see our familiar faces as it is for us to see them come back again and again. But, perhaps, I'm just defining what a friend is." — Vermont

"Our winter season began well but the February rain succeeded in ending the season early. Even so, we had some interesting things occur in that short space of time. One night our power went out at 7 p.m. and we had 75 for dinner. We served by candle and little cautious steps. As we cook by gas the food stayed hot. The power came back at 2 a.m. and my son and I did dishes until 3:30 a.m. When the temperature went to 35° below and remained there 24 hours our gas line froze so we ended up doing breakfast for sixty on our newly installed wood stove." — New York

"I must say that it is very satisfying to find our inn guests gathered in the TV-sitting room getting acquainted over a ball game. So many people from all over the country come to visit here and they have so much to offer. It just amazes me how a house full of people can become one big happy family. I guess that is what innkeeping is all about. What fun it is!!" — New Hampshire

"Thanks to your meeting last year and Tom and Peggy Wright of Redcoat's Return, we are now using their roast duckling with great success. Sarah and I always enjoy your meetings as a real learning experience and we have brought back many good ideas (not to mention curtains) from every meeting that we have been able to attend." — Ontario, Canada

Continued on page 54

To Jane and Pete Johnston

Contents

UNITED STATES

(*) Asterisk denotes inn listed for first time in 1982

(*) Asterisk denotes inn listed for first time in 1982

(*) Asterisk denotes inn listed for first time in 1982

CANADA

To our readers in Great Britain and other countries in Europe:

Welcome to North America! Many of you are making your first visit and we're delighted that you'll be experiencing some of the *real* United States and Canada by visiting these country inns. Incidentally, all of them will be very happy to help you make arrangements and reservations at other inns in the book.

For your further convenience, automobile rental reservations for the United States can be made before your departure through a world-wide rental corporation: AutoEurope.

Here are some AutoEurope telephone numbers in major European cities to make easy contact before departing: Brussels: 649-9524; Copenhagen: 153636; Paris: 2733520; Munich: 223333; Athens: 9225718; Amsterdam: 178505; Rome: 4756412; Luxemburg: 435049; Lisbon: 884257; Madrid: 2341004; Stockholm: 231070; Zurich: 425656; London: 2934-74-123; Ireland, Shannon: 61 61 532; Ireland, Dublin: 61671.

Once in North America, the toll-free telephone number for AutoEurope is 1-800-223-5555.

Are you using old editions of Country Inns and Back Roads, North America? *Please don't. Like railway timetables, they are bound to become increasingly out-of-date each year. Since there are several new recommendations each year and several previous ones are omitted, may I suggest that you take any outdated copy to any of the inns featured in this book and the innkeeper will be happy to exchange your copy for a brand new 1982 edition.*

I do not include lodging rates in the descriptions, for the very nature of an inn means that there are lodgings of various sizes, with and without baths, in and out of season, and with plain and fancy decoration. Travelers should call ahead and inquire about the availability and rates of the many different types of rooms.

"European Plan" means that rates for rooms and meals are separate. "American Plan" means that meals are included in the cost of the room. "Modified American Plan" means that breakfast and dinner are included in the cost of the room. The rates at some inns include a continental breakfast with the lodging.

MONTREAL

North Hero House, *North Hero*

Inn on the Common,
● *Craftsbury Common*

■ BURLINGTON

Philbrook Farm, *Shelburne*

Rabbit Hill Inn, *Lower Waterford* ● Spalding Inn,
ST. JOHNSBURY ■ ● *Whitefield*

V E R M O N T

Dana Place Inn, *Jackson*

Lovett's, *Franconia*
NORTH CONWAY

Rockhouse Mountain Farm, *Eaton Center*
Darby Field Inn, *Conway* ●
Stafford's-In-The-Field, *Chocorua* ●

Blueberry Hill Farm, *Goshen*
● Lyme Inn, *Lyme*

RUTLAND ■ Kedron Valley Inn,
South Woodstock ● ■ HANOVER
Middletown Springs Inn, Quechee Inn
Middletown Springs *Quechee*
● Hickory Stick
Farm, *Laconia*

Barrows House, Village Inn, *Landgrove*
Dorset ● ● *Inn at Weathersfield, Weathersfield*
● Chester Inn, *Chester* ● Dexter's Inn, *Sunapee*
● Birch Hill Inn, *Manchester* N E W
● Three Mountain Inn, ■ CONCORD
Jamaica H A M P S H I R E
Old Newfane Inn, ● Colby Hill Inn, *Henniker*
Newfane ●
Inn at Sawmill Farm, Inn at Crotched Mt., *Francestown*
West Dover ● John Hancock Inn, *Hancock*
Woodbound, *Jaffrey*
●

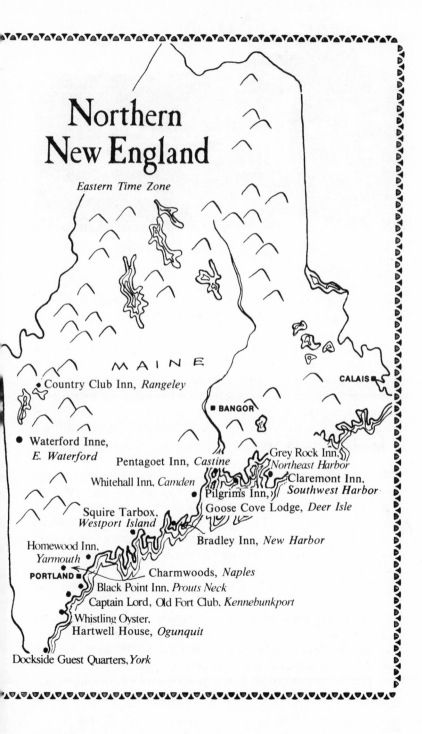

Northern
New England

Eastern Time Zone

M A I N E

CALAIS ■

• Country Club Inn, *Rangeley*

■ BANGOR

● Waterford Inne,
   E. Waterford

Pentagoet Inn, *Castine*

Grey Rock Inn,
Northeast Harbor

Whitehall Inn, *Camden*

Claremont Inn,
Southwest Harbor

● Pilgrim's Inn,

Squire Tarbox,
Westport Island

Goose Cove Lodge, *Deer Isle*

Homewood Inn,
Yarmouth ●

Bradley Inn, *New Harbor*

PORTLAND ■

Charmwoods, *Naples*

Black Point Inn, *Prouts Neck*

Captain Lord, Old Fort Club, *Kennebunkport*

Whistling Oyster,
Hartwell House, *Ogunquit*

Dockside Guest Quarters, *York*

Maine

THE WATERFORD INNE
East Waterford, Maine

"We're such a tiny inn," said Barbara Vanderzanden as she set down the tray with some teacups, "that we personally speak to *every* guest who stays with us. As you see everybody is drawn together in our living room and oftentimes we spend the entire evening with our guests chatting or playing bridge. Because we are small our guests get to know one another, too. Many nights they are all seated together at the dinner table and we can hear them exchanging addresses for future visits. Recently two couples got together to make reservations for the next *CIBR* inn to be visited the following evening. Two couples met here in the summer last year and returned to spend New Year's Eve."

At The Waterford Inne, located in the little-known Oxford Hills area of western Maine, "small and tidy" is beautiful. The original house was built in 1825 and has five upstairs bedrooms that step out of the 19th century. These were augmented by four additional rooms created in a wing leading to a very large barn. A recent addition to the building by Barbara and her mother Rosalie has provided greater convenience for the kitchen chores, and also for Barbara and Rosalie's own personal space. Jan Lindstrom's new sketch of the inn shows how well it balances off the remainder of the house.

Innkeeping responsibilities are divided between this mother-daughter team, both of whom had been schoolteachers from Oradel, New Jersey. "Mother is the real creative force in the kitchen," said Barbara, as we settled down in the main living room with its warm barnboards and views of the hills in two directions. "She's developed some wonderful recipes and does all the cooking. I do the serving and the two of us pitch right in and take care of all the other chores in the house.

"We serve a fixed-price dinner every evening for both house-guests and visitors. We do all our own baking and in season use only fresh vegetables from our garden. Often there's less than an hour between picking and eating!

"Cross-country skiing is very popular here," Rosalie continued. "We have some trails leading from our own property into the woods and beyond. People also bring their own snowshoes. In warmer weather, there are dozens of diversions."

Rosalie excused herself to run into the kitchen and Barbara went out to greet some new guests, leaving me the opportunity to contemplate the many books and periodicals. There was also a whole shelf filled with such parlor games as backgammon, checkers, and chess. The coffee table carved out of natural wood was also a cribbage board, and in one corner an old buggy seat was piled high with magazines.

Rosalie returned with a letter in her hand, saying, "Here's a letter from one of our guests that I thought you'd find interesting." The letter read in part, "After our visit with you I feel as if we've been friends for years—something very rare indeed in this hectic and sometimes uncaring world that we live in."

THE WATERFORD INNE, Box 49, East Waterford, Maine 04233; 207-583-4037. A 9-room farmhouse-inn in the Oxford Hills section of southwest Maine, 8 mi. from Norway and South Paris. Closed March and April. Breakfast and dinner served to travelers by reservation. European plan. Within a short distance of many recreational, scenic, and cultural attractions in Maine and the White Mountains of New Hampshire. Cross-country skiing and badminton on grounds. Lake swimming, golf, rock hunting, downhill skiing, hiking, canoeing nearby. No credit cards. Alcoholic beverages not served. Well-behaved pets welcome; however, advance notification is required and a fee is charged. Rosalie and Barbara Vanderzanden, Innkeepers.

Directions: From Maine Turnpike: use Exit 11, follow Rte. 26 north approximately 28 mi. into Norway, then on Rte. 118 west for 8 mi. to Rte. 37 south (left turn). Go ½ mi., turn right at Springer's General Store, up the hill ½ mi. From Conway, New Hampshire: Rte. 16 to Rte. 302 east to Fryeburg, Me. Take Rte. 5 out of Fryeburg to Rte. 35 south, thence to Rte. 118, which is a left fork (with Rte. 35 going right). Continue on Rte. 118 east, past Papoose Pond camping area, then watch for right turn onto Rte. 37. Go ½ mi. to Springer's General Store. Take immediate right turn, ½ mi. up hill.

CAPTAIN LORD MANSION
Kennebunkport, Maine

This time I arrived at the Captain Lord Mansion early in September to find Rick attending to Dana Dale Litchfield, who at that time was nine or ten months old, and Beverly looking positively beautiful and informing me that another little innkeeper would be in residence when the readers of this book make visits in 1982. Meanwhile, Dana was ruling the roost and Rick said she loved going *up* the stairs, but could not at that point manage to come down. "The guests are all her friends," he said. "She is really 'Miss Personality plus.'"

The Captain Lord Mansion provides an opportunity for guests to be transported into an elegant era of the 19th century. It is an imposing three-story building topped by a most impressive cupola. There are at least thirty-five rooms in the mansion, sixteen have been set aside as lodging rooms and all of them have their own private baths. To make the prospect even more inviting, eleven of these rooms have working fireplaces.

In addition to the cupola, the original structure claims one of the few three-story, unsupported, elliptical staircases in Maine. Each stately, blown-glass window is considerably enhanced by hand-sewn draperies. The window frames of the front rooms of the first two stories have double Indian shutters. The beautiful floors with their original pine boards are a handsome complement to the furnishings, most of which are antiques of great history and pedigree.

Since 1978 Bev and Rick have made significant improvements in the quality and the diversification of hospitality presented to their guests. There are posturepedic mattresses, thick carpets, color-coordinated linens, and lovely works of art. Fluffy comforters, homemade quilts, or 100% wool blankets provide extra warmth against those cold Maine nights. In order to accommodate those who prefer oversized beds there are three rooms with queen-sized and three rooms with king-sized beds. I'm almost sure that it's impossible for anyone to run out of hot water, because four 82-gallon water heaters have now been installed.

All of the lodging rooms are named for ships built by Nathanial Lord or his sons. Each has a history that tells when and where the ship was built, the first captain, the principal owner, and the date it was launched.

Breakfast at the Captain Lord Mansion is served in the warm, inviting kitchen, where Bev and Rick and the assistant manager Nancy Blanchard bustle around serving pumpkin, zucchini, and cranberry bread, various types of coffeecakes and cinnamon rolls, as well as soft-boiled eggs, juice, and coffee or tea. In the wintertime, breakfast is served in bed to those who request it.

Here's an excerpt from a letter I received last fall: "Bev and Rick are true innkeepers— from the warm greeting to each guest and eagerness to answer questions, to the delicious breakfast. We had never stayed in an inn or a hotel where a room on the second floor had its own private elevator from the first floor. One of the things that impressed us was the fact that there was a whole linen press full of games for the guests to enjoy. We met a couple at breakfast and discovered that we were all game-players, so that evening we got together in the living room and tried several games. It was hard to leave such a restful place with such friendly hosts."

Just before this book went to the printers I received word that Stacia Ann Litchfield, a healthy seven-pound, thirteen-ounce girl had been born on January 21st at 6 a.m.

THE CAPTAIN LORD MANSION, Box 527, Kennebunkport, Me. 04046; 207-967-3141. A 16-bedroom inn located in a mansion in a seacoast village. Lodgings include breakfast. No other meals served. Open year-round. Near the Rachel Carson Wildlife Refuge, the Seashore Trolley Museum, The Brick Store Museum, and lobster boat tours. Bicycles, hiking, xc skiing, deep sea fishing, golf, indoor swimming, and tennis nearby. No children under 12. No pets. No credit cards. Bev Davis and Rick Litchfield, Innkeepers.

Directions: Take Exit 3 (Kennebunk) from the Maine Turnpike. Take left on Rte. 35 and follow signs through Kennebunk to Kennebunkport. Take left at traffic light at Sunoco station. Go over drawbridge and take first right onto Ocean Ave., then take fourth left after Texaco. The mansion is on the second block on left. Park behind building and take brick walk to office.

THE CLAREMONT HOTEL AND COTTAGES
Southwest Harbor, Maine

The tide was out but the fleet was in as I walked down the broad lawn once again to the Boat House at the Claremont, and saw that the new volleyball net had been erected and a croquet game was already in progress, as the championships at Claremont were being held over the coming weekend.

Meanwhile on the waters of Somes Sound, there were at least eight or nine beautiful sailboats moored, their white masts sharply in contrast to the green hills on the other side. Oddly enough, my previous visits to the Claremont always seemed to be when the tide was in. This time, the bare rocks and the shore life they supported made a very interesting and striking scene.

Innkeeper Jay Madeira and I were seated on the lawn of the Claremont which has been a resort inn for almost a hundred years. It is the oldest continuously operating hotel on the island. In recent years, the McCue family has added attractive cottages which are nestled in the trees with a view of the water. "There have been more visitors from Europe," he said, "particularly from England. Many people fly to Bangor which is fifty miles away, or to Bar Harbor, which is eleven, and we pick them up. Many of our guests are coming in the early or late season, and we've adjusted our schedule for people who might enjoy Mount Desert Island when almost no one but year-round residents are here."

The Claremont opened in the summer of 1884 and has known only three owners in all of its years, which in itself is most unusual. Successive generations have been returning ever since the inn opened, although the Claremont has become more and more a place for vacationing families and honeymooners. Its designation to the National Register of Historic Places reads: "A reminder of Maine's early summer resort period of the 1870s and '80s . . . of a prosperous, relaxed and seasonal way of life."

There are twenty-two rooms in the three-story main building with additional rooms in the Phillips House, the Clark House, and other cottages.

One of the reasons for its continuing popularity is the extensive menu prepared by chef Billie McIntire, who is now in her eighth year at Claremont and has received well-deserved national recognition for her talents. Besides the lobster, scallops, steak, and tournedos, the seafood crepes have been popular. The desserts are fabulous. Many a resolve goes out the window when guests see something being served at the next table.

Ever since my first visit here, I've been struck by the wide variety of entertainment and recreation that the Claremont guests can enjoy. For example, the location on Mount Desert Island puts all of the wonderful attractions of the area within a very convenient distance.

The Claremont approaches its one hundredth year with great anticipation.

THE CLAREMONT HOTEL AND COTTAGES, Southwest Harbor, Me. 04679; 207-244-5036. A 22-room rambling summer hotel with rooms also in two adjacent guest houses; on Somes Sound, Mt. Desert Island, 24 mi. south of Ellsworth. Modified American plan omits lunch. All rooms with private baths except two with shared baths. Hotel opens June 18 to Sept. 19. Guest house rooms available March through Nov. Nine housekeeping cottages on grounds open May 15 to Oct. 15. Dining room open June 18 to Sept. 20 serving dinner and breakfast daily to the public as well as guests, and open for dinner only through Sept. 30th. Tennis, rowboats, croquet, badminton, dock and deepwater moorings on grounds. Fresh water swimming, golf, bicycles, riding, boating, and sailing rental nearby. No credit cards. Personal checks accepted. The McCue Family, Owners; John Madeira, Jr., Manager.

Directions: From Maine Tpke., exit at Augusta and proceed east on Rte. 3 to US #1. At Ellsworth, pick up Rte. 3 again and follow Rte. 102 on Mt. Desert Island to Southwest Harbor. Follow inn signs approaching and in Southwest Harbor.

GOOSE COVE LODGE
Deer Isle, Maine

I couldn't believe it. Once again, almost a year later, to the day, I was trotting behind Elli Pavloff doing my best not to appear out of breath and feeling a little bit like either Lewis or Clark as they followed the Indian maiden through the wilds of the Northwest. Last year she had taken me to *all* of the accommodations at Goose Cove Lodge—the cabins and the cottages—and pointed out that almost

every lodging room has a fireplace, and that they were all originally built so that each and every one affords a gorgeous view of Goose Cove.

Today, we were on one of the many nature walks that starts from the lodge and plunges into the woods, coming out on the rocky shore. After a few minutes of scrambling along behind her, I came out to a formation of wonderful pink granite rocks overlooking Penobscot Bay, and Elli pointed across to North Haven Island and beyond to the famous mountain at Camden where Edna St. Vincent Millay found such inspiration. She indicated a little spit of land to the north that was the town of Castine. In front of us were dozens of lobster pots bobbing on the relatively serene water.

We sat on the rocks for a moment and Elli said, "Goose Cove appeals to so many different kinds of people. We have honeymooners, senior citizens, and middle-aged folks like you and me who are beginning to creak a little. But we also have young families. It is a combination of the really spectacular beauty of the place, its privacy, and the fellowship of the gatherings in lodge, that combine to make everything a unique experience. I think the simplicity of the cottages brings the out-of-doors and nature closer to the guests. I guess I'm rhapsodizing, but this is one of the very special places with a magic all its own, and there aren't many places that are still unspoiled. We love Goose Cove. I know I'm going to miss it even while we're in France this winter, but I'll be looking forward to next spring and summer's innkeeping adventures."

We walked on farther and crossed the sandbar to Barred Island, a nature conservancy, which is accessible only at low tide. "One of our expert birdwatcher-guests drew up a list in July of over 100 different birds spotted on the lodge grounds," she said. "Several people have seen a bobcat, and baby foxes and deer may appear in September. It's quite common to see jack rabbits and other furred or quilled creatures."

Goose Cove Lodge is on the modified American plan and all guests take breakfast and dinner in the dining room. Box lunches or sandwiches which can be eaten on the beach or on the trails are cheerfully prepared by the dining room staff. Everyone gathers at the end of the day in the lodge before dinner for some of Elli's superb hors d'oeuvres and this is where the beautiful new friendships are made.

The Athena of innkeepers stood up and began striding up the beach. "The fall is lovely here," she remarked. "I wish I could preserve some of it for the summer folk to see. There's clear blue sky, blue water, dark green pines, orange leaves—a symphony of color. By the way, we're going to have seven housekeeping cottages available next year starting May first and we are not closing until October fifteenth." I made a mental note.

GOOSE COVE LODGE, Sunset, Deer Isle, Me. 04683; 207-348-2508. A 22-room (60 people) resort-inn on beautiful Penobscot Bay approx. 1½ hrs. from Rte. 1 at Bucksport. Open May 1 to Oct. 15. Modified American plan. Meals served to houseguests only. Swimming, boating, canoeing, hiking, and birdwatching all available at the inn. Other outdoor sports, including backroading, golf, tennis, etc., nearby. Especially adaptable for children of all ages. Elli and George Pavloff, Innkeepers.

Directions: From Rte. 1 follow Rte. 15 north to Deer Isle Village, turn right on Sunset. Proceed 3 miles. Turn right at Goose Cove Rd. (marked by sign). Follow road 1½ miles to the end.

PILGRIM'S INN
Deer Isle, Maine

Travelers really have to be looking for Deer Isle and Pilgrim's Inn. It's thirty miles down from coastal Route 1 running between Bucksport and Ellsworth, along the Blue Hill Peninsula, across Eggemoggin Reach on the old suspension bridge to Little Deer, along the snaking causeway to Deer Isle, and then a few miles more to the village.

Spoken of locally as "The Harbor," the village of Deer Isle is one block long at its business center and Pilgrim's Inn stands at the far end of this block. The inn is a four-storied gambrel-roofed great

house, since 1793 overlooking a long harbor in front and a large millpond to the rear.

Inside the front door there is a formal parlor on the left which is the original dining room, and to the right the more homey and cluttered parlor of the innkeepers.

Standing in the hallway, the chances are the traveler will hear someone call, "Come on downstairs." This is the real heart and the most populated part of the inn since it contains the kitchen, dining room, old taproom, common room, and library. George Pavloff is quite likely to be there, along with one or more of the staff. A tour of the inn is offered.

The eleven guest bedrooms are mostly quite large and little changed from the colonial days of Squire Haskell. There are richly hued pine floorboards, a woodstove, a queen-sized bed, old wooden furniture, and an unusual selection of books and magazines in each bedroom. Baths are semi-private and Elli Pavloff says, "Six are a lot more than they had in 1793!"

At about six o'clock in the evening every day, the Common Room becomes the center of attraction and conversation for everyone. Dinner is served in the barn dining room, after which some guests stroll the waterfront, while others return to the Common Room for games, music, and conversation.

There might be entertainment during dinner because there are many gifted musicians in the area. On my last visit there were two guitar-playing singers who offered pleasant folk songs in many languages.

Guests may also make arrangements to dine at Goose Cove Lodge, where Elli Pavloff is more likely to be found, since she and George own both places.

"Do nothing pleasantly," is at the top of the list of activities in the inn's brochure. "This is not the place for anyone in a hurry," says George. "Before Labor Day guests make reservations well in advance and stay long enough to rest and to explore our area. After Labor Day very many of them phone only a day in advance. They are on the road with their *CIBR*'s inn-hopping like grasshoppers, generally staying for one night only.

"People seem a bit frantic in their desire to see everything before going home for the winter. Elli and I feel that one-night stays are not really good for vacationing guests; we suggest that rather than going from place to place each day, seeing much, enjoying and savoring little, ending up agitated rather than rested and at peace, they pick one or two places, even if ours is not included, go there and *STAY*. Relax, let go, smell the local roses and depart really refreshed with new friends, and perhaps a few new pounds, ready for the fray again."

PILGRIM'S INN, Deer Isle, Me. 04627; 207-348-6615. An 11-room inn, some with shared baths, in a remote island village on the Blue Hill Peninsula on the Maine coast. Modified American plan, May 15 to Nov. 1, includes a hearty breakfast and a gourmet dinner. During the winter, bed and breakfast is offered to the passing pilgrim. In season outside dinner reservations accepted Wednesdays through Saturdays. A 4-day minimum reservation is required in August. Bicycles, badminton, ping-pong, regulation horseshoes, croquet, and a rowboat for the millpond on the grounds. The Deer Isle area is replete with all types of cultural and recreational advantages including golf, fishing, sailing, hiking, and browsing. George and Eleanor Pavloff, Innkeepers.

Directions: From Boston, take I-95 to Brunswick exit. Take coastal Rte. 1 south past Bucksport. Turn right on Rte. 15 which travels to Deer Isle down the Blue Hill Peninsula. At the village, turn right on Main Street (Sunset Rd.) and proceed one block to the Inn on the left side of the street, opposite the Harbor.

DOCKSIDE GUEST QUARTERS
York, Maine

"If you'll just cast off, Norman, we'll head out through the harbor and into the Atlantic!"

This was going to be a real treat for me because David Lusty was taking his mother Lois and me, along with several inn guests, on a pleasant excursion that would provide all of us with some exceptional views of York harbor and some of the beautiful homes that border it.

It was an outstanding morning in late September. The sun was sparkling on the water and we were for a short time convoyed by a group of ducklings, a part of the regular harbor contingent of mallards, while the gulls swept overhead. The white pines, firs, and native spruces which remain green throughout the year were intermixed with crimsons and oranges, as well as with the rusty greens of the hickory, sumac, and beech trees.

I've always tried to arrange to visit this part of lower Maine in late September or during the early days of October because the combination of the fall colors and the waterside atmosphere make it such an enjoyable experience.

Our craft was called the *Not Me*. I think it's the direct result of David's Puckish sense of humor and is explained by the fact that there are four boys in the Lusty family and when anyone was accused of some misdeed all would reply in a chorus, "not me." The other derivation of the name is the fact that the boat was really made in Nova Scotia, so that it is not Me. It took me a little while to figure that one out, too.

The Dockside Guest Quarters includes the original New England homestead of the 1880s, called the Maine House, and other cottage buildings of a contemporary design, each with its own porch and water view. Some have a casual studio feeling.

The innkeepers are David and Harriette Lusty. David is a real "State of Maine" man, complete with a wonderful down-east accent. They met in college and were themselves married at Dockside Guest Quarters, so the precedents for honeymoons have been well established.

As we headed out of the river, David pointed to a large orange mark on the shoreline cliff. "We have now crossed into the Atlantic Ocean," he said. "It's against the law to fish for lobsters in the York

River, but it is OK to put the lobster pots down out here," he said, indicating the dozens and dozens of bobbing markers.

He cut off the motor and pointed out a number of beautiful homes along the shoreline. "Incidentally, we have a Cliff Walk in York Harbor similar to the Marginal Way in Ogunquit," he said. "Many of our guests enjoy the self-guided walking or motoring maps of York which provide a wonderful overview of the history of the area."

Late September and early October days in York can be spent in many different ways. There are a number of sandy beaches and swimming can be excellent when the sun is highest at midday and early afternoon. Other times it's great fun to wander along these stretches of beach and have them almost entirely to oneself. Golf and tennis are available at the golf club, the marina has rental sailboats and outboards, and guests can also visit Strawberry Banke in nearby Portsmouth.

A few years ago David and Harriette added the Dockside dining room, managed by Steve and Sue Roeder, where luncheon and dinner are served, with a great many seafood specialities. One of the features of the menu is roast duckling à la Hickory Stick, which originated at the Hickory Stick Farm in Laconia, New Hampshire. Incidentally, since my last visit, John Powers, the chef, and Joanne Lees, who runs the gift shop at Dockside, were married on board the excursion steamer which plies the waters of Lake Winnipesaukee. "The wedding party took the entire ship," said David.

DOCKSIDE GUEST QUARTERS, P.O. Box 205, Harris Island Rd., York, Me. 03909; 207-363-2868. An 18-room waterside country inn 10 mi. from Portsmouth, N.H. Some studio suites in newer multiunit cottages. York Village is a National Historic District. American plan available. Continental breakfast served to houseguests only. Dockside Dining Room serves lunch and dinner to travelers daily except Mondays. Open from Memorial Day weekend in May through Columbus Day. Lawn games, shuffleboard and badminton, fishing, sailing, and boating from premises. Golf, tennis, and swimming nearby; safe and picturesque paths and roadways for walks, bicycling, and jogging. Credit cards are accepted for amounts up to fifty dollars. Personal checks accepted for payment of food and lodgings incurred by registered guests. David and Harriette Lusty, Innkeepers.

Directions: From U.S. 1 or I-95, take Exit at York to Rte. 1A. Follow 1A thru center of old York Village, take Rte. 103 (a side street off Rte. 1A leading to the harbor), and watch for signs to the inn.

THE WHISTLING OYSTER
Ogunquit, Maine

It is most gratifying for me to realize how many years I've been visiting The Whistling Oyster restaurant on Perkins Cove in Ogunquit, Maine; I've been sharing my lunches and dinners with readers of *CIBR* since the late 1960s.

I am most fortunate to have known Mr. John Parella during all these years, and he and I often recall the early days when he was still on the faculty of the Music School at Temple University in Philadelphia, and was a commuting innkeeper and voice instructor.

On this particular visit, John and I once again were looking out over the waters of Perkins Cove where the lobster boats were coming in under the drawbridge and many smaller boats darted among the moored pleasure craft.

This time John was filled with the news about the new chef. "His name is Michael Allen. He comes to us directly from the Henri IV restaurant in Cambridge, and his credentials are tremendous. His awards include International Food and Wine Society's Certificate of Excellence; Confrerie des Chevaliers du Tastevin's Award of Excellence; and Boston Magazine's 'Best French Restaurant.' He studied French cuisine, both classic and nouvelle, with Madeleine Kamman, and he has received top reviews from the Boston Globe and the Boston Herald American."

Meanwhile, the waiter had served our lunch and this time I forsook my usual order of crabmeat Snug Harbor for an order of eggs Benedict which looked almost too good to eat. Our conversation swung around to the best times to visit Maine. "Oh, to me June and September are just wonderful," John said. "It's considerably less crowded and there's more elbow room and more fun. By the way," he said, "have you ever walked the Marginal Way? You know if you really want to feel close and intimate with the sea, this is *the* thing to do for visitors in Ogunquit. The path works its way along the rocky shore and it's a wonderful experience with the movement of the waves and the swooping of gulls overhead."

I would like to share a letter I received from Rick and Bev Litchfield at the nearby Captain Lord's Mansion in Kennebunkport. It says in part, "The Whistling Oyster was closed in January when we were making plans for our wedding a few years ago, so we went to another restaurant. Forty-eight hours before we were to arrive, the restaurant could not meet our needs. At 9:30 in the evening we called John and asked if there was any way he could accommodate thirty people for our wedding party and dinner. He called back after consulting the chef, and the plans were all confirmed that evening.

"Our dinner was superb. John and his maitre d' served us personally and nothing could have been more perfect. We're so happy and will always feel a warm glow towards John Parella and the Whistling Oyster."

When I reminded John of that incident, he gave his staff credit. "Actually," he said, "I think it's one of the reasons we decided to remain open in the wintertime and got into a program of international dinners."

One further note: the parking lot for The Whistling Oyster is not the parking lot immediately across from the restaurant itself. Go another fifty yards or so farther, turn left, and follow the road about 100 yards to the Whistling Oyster parking sign.

THE WHISTLING OYSTER, Perkins Cove, Ogunquit, Me. 03907; 207-646-9521. A waterfront restaurant in Perkins Cove at Ogunquit. No lodgings. Lunch and dinner served daily. Open throughout the year. Reservations advisable. Nearby CIBR *overnight lodgings can be found at The Hartwell House, Ogunquit (207-646-7210). John Parella, Innkeeper.*

Directions: From the south, take the York exit from I-95. Turn north on Rte. 1 to Ogunquit Square. Proceed south on Shore Rd. for about 1 mi. to Perkins Cove turnoff.

HOMEWOOD INN
Yarmouth, Maine

Perhaps more than the ceremony itself, the most poignant moment was the short few seconds afterward when Julie Webster set aside the happy days of her late childhood and early adult life here at the Homewood Inn and stepped forward into the future as Mrs. Andrew Frank.

Earlier in the day I had hastened down the Maine coast, leaving Blue Hill to reach Yarmouth and the Homewood Inn in time for the

wedding. I had known Julie for a number of years and this was an occasion not to be missed.

The wedding ceremony took place on a little knoll on the inn grounds underneath two lovely pine trees with the background of the waters of Casco Bay in one direction and the lovely Maine coast meadows and fields in the other. During the time that the vows were being given, a sweet little chickadee alighted on one of the pine branches. Meanwhile, the gentle and pervasive sounds of a lute wafted over the scene. It seemed so lovely, natural, and so right for dear Julie to be married in the setting that she loved and which would always be part of her life.

Then, of course, there were the congratulations and the photographs and the cutting of the cake and the giggles and hugs and kisses from Fred and Colleen Webster, her father and mother, and the proud feelings radiating from her grandmother, Doris Gillette and her husband, Ted. I felt so wonderful and privileged to be invited to this small family wedding and to be among these people that I have known and loved at such an important time.

Now came the golden moment. Julie, looking radiant in a lovely dress, gathered the bridesmaids and other single girls, all equally attractive in their summer dresses, and prepared to toss the bouquet. She turned her back and everyone watched to see who would catch it and be the next bride. Julie threw the bouquet over her head and everybody "oohed" and then cheered as it was caught by Julie's young grandniece, Madeline Yale. Everyone laughed, and someone said, "If all of those girls have to wait for Madeline to get married before it's their turn, there are going to be quite a few spinsters around here!"

I must confess there was a lump in my throat as I wandered away from the wedding party past the tennis courts and the swimming pool and threaded my way among the many single and double cottages which make up most of the inn complex. These are set among the juniper, cedar and Norway pines. Once again, I was attracted to the multitude of flowers, including roses, phlox, snapdragons, and marigolds. I walked out on the wooden dock and sat down in the warm late afternoon sunshine. It was a very singular day, indeed.

(P.S.: I learned later that Julie and Andrew had gone to Lovett's Inn in Franconia, New Hampshire, where they enjoyed a splendid three-day honeymoon.)

HOMEWOOD INN, Drinkwater Point, Yarmouth, Me. 04096; 207-846-3351. A 46-room waterside inn in Casco Bay north of Portland. European plan. Breakfast and dinner served to travelers daily except Mondays when continental breakfast and steak or lobster cookout at night available (by advance reservation). Open June 11 through October 12. (Some rooms and cottages with kitchenettes available from mid-May and after mid-October.) Bicycles (incl. tandems), pool, tennis, croquet court, boating, hiking, salt water swimming on grounds. Golf, riding, fishing, state parks, theater nearby. Fred, Colleen, and Julie Webster, Ted and Doris Gillette, Innkeepers.

Directions: From the south, take Exit 9 from Maine Tpke. (I-95) to Rte. 1-N, or Exit 17 from I-295 to Rte. 1-N, and follow signs to inn. From north (Brunswick area) from I-95, take "Yarmouth, Rte. 1" exit and follow signs to the inn.

BLACK POINT INN
Prouts Neck, Maine

Under a brilliant Maine August sun, on my last trip to the Black Point Inn, I set out after breakfast to walk the Prouts Neck path. The usual course is to follow the path directly from the front of the inn. However, this time I decided to walk counter-clockwise and wound my way up through the beautiful trees and cottages that make up the private residential area of the community. Most of these are built of brown, weathered shingles with white trim, the same design as the inn. Some of the same families have been summering here for generations.

Following Norm Dugas's directions, I cut through to the ocean at a point where I could see the Winslow Homer Studio, and then started walking in the marshlands and thickets beside the sea. Eventually, the path came out on the rocks and led to the sandy beach favored by inn guests who like chilly salt water.

The path came out on a ledge above the sea, and I stretched out on the warm rock and began to muse about the conversation I had had a dinner the night before when Norm had mentioned the fact that

Prouts Neck was first settled about 1630, and in 1690, the trouble with the French and Indians caused the colonists to leave it for twelve years. In 1702, they started a new trading post. However, in 1713, nineteen men were ambushed and killed by Indians at the southern end of Massacre Pond, which is just across the road from the Prouts Neck golf course.

"It became popular as a summer resort in the middle of the 19th century," he pointed out. "In 1886 there were a half dozen summer cottages. One of them was occupied by Charles Savage Homer whose son, Winslow, became one of America's most well-known artists. He must have gotten his inspiration for some of those great paintings of the Maine coast from just walking on the rocks and the beaches here."

It was now about twelve noon and I could hear the tuning-up of the small orchestra that plays both for the poolside buffet at noon, and for dancing after dinner at the inn. Incidentally, there is lobster on the menu every day.

The Black Point Inn is one of the few remaining American plan hotels that flourished in New England for about 100 years. It has quiet dignity, personal service, attention to details, ocean bathing, excellent tennis courts, a golf course, exceptional food, and an unpretentious elegance. Men wear coats for dinner and many of the ladies enjoy wearing their gay, summer dresses. Dressing up is part of the fun. That is the way it has been ever since I have been visiting this inn which, like the Spalding Inn in Whitefield, New Hampshire, provides one of the last few remaining intimate resort-inn experiences.

It is worth noting the "social season" runs from the last weekend in June to Labor Day and that before and after this period, services are somewhat curtailed because there are group meetings at the inn, and menu planning and other services are adjusted to meet their needs. Norm Dugas makes a point that they're happy to take transient guests in late September or October, but do have many motorcoach tours at that time and he wants everybody to know the dining room can become rather noisy.

BLACK POINT INN, Prouts Neck, Me. 04070; 207-883-4311. An 80-room luxury resort-inn on Rte. 207, 10 mi. south of Portland. American plan. Breakfast, lunch, and dinner served to travelers. Open May 20 to Oct. 12. Fresh water whirlpool, heated salt water pool, bicycles, sailing, dancing, golf, tennis, and ocean bathing all within a few steps. No pets. Normand H. Dugas, Innkeeper.

Directions: From Maine Tpke., take Exit 7. Turn right at sign marked Scarborough and Old Orchard Beach. At second set of lights turn left on Rte. 207. Follow 4.3 miles to Prouts Neck.

WHITEHALL INN
Camden, Maine

I'd like to share some portions of a letter I received from a reader who lives in Billerica, Massachusetts. She is telling about her visit to the Whitehall Inn:

"The inn was humming with activity when I arrived—parking places were few and far between, but I squeezed my mid-sized car between a lamp post and an Audi with Illinois license plates. This was obviously a popular place for guests and natives alike. Even so, as busy as they were, they managed to find an empty table for me where I sat and drank in my surroundings. The lights were low, Mozart filled the air, the candles glimmered behind cut-glass holders which in turn reflected the light a hundred times over. Flowers leaned gently on the rims of their vases and all of these things made for a softly elegant, quietly enjoyable evening. The meal and service were both excellent. I left the dining room with a nicely full, nicely relaxed feeling.

"To my delight, Camden had already begun to change from its green summer uniform to its gold and red autumn wardrobe. Sitting atop Mt. Battie, camera slung over one shoulder, binoculars over the other, I didn't know which to reach for first as the sun broke through the morning haze scattering light over the bay below setting it a-shimmering like a basketful of precious gems. A Windjammer sailed gracefully into view, its many sails filled with enough wind to carry it smoothly and serenely to the harbor. Such peace, such tranquility, such perfection—all here this day in Camden, Maine.

"I ventured forth into Camden State Park and later walked

around the village finding many new and exciting things in the shops.

"Later back at the inn I struck up the acquaintance of some other guests and noted a couple playing checkers in one corner of the lobby. I reached for one of the many worn leatherbound books and chose a Dickens novel, the pages of which were yellowed with age and dog-eared from obvious constant use.

"Mr. Dewing inquired after my day's activities and was interested in hearing how I had bided my time in a town he obviously loves a great deal.

"Next morning I was invited to eat breakfast with my new friends and we had a lovely conversation over blueberry griddle cakes, spicy sausages, and cold, fresh orange juice."

There is little I can add to this account of a lovely visit to the Whitehall Inn in Camden, except to say that the Dewings continue to prosper with all three of their now-grown children involved in the inn during the summer. The biggest news is that Chip Dewing was married on January 16th to Kathy Bertolino who has been a member of the Whitehall staff for five years, and we all wish them well.

In closing, let me say that if I publish many more letters like the one above, I might find myself out of a job.

WHITEHALL INN, Camden, Me. 04843; 207-236-3391. A 38-room village inn in a Maine seacoast town, 75 mi. from Portland. Modified American plan omits lunch. Breakfast and dinner served daily to travelers. Open, May 25 to Oct. 15. Tennis, bicycles, shuffleboard, day sailing, harbor cruises on grounds. Golf, hiking, swimming, fishing nearby. No pets. Jean and Ed Dewing, Innkeepers.

Directions: From Maine Tpke. take Exit 9 to coastal Rte. 95. Proceed on 95 to Rte. 1 at Brunswick. Follow Rte. 1 to Rte. 90 at Warren, to Rte. 1 in Camden. Inn is located on Rte. 1, ¼ mi. north of Camden.

SQUIRE TARBOX INN
Westport Island, Maine

I was driving north up the coast of Maine on U.S. Route 1. I passed through Bath and started looking for Route 144, which turns off the main road on the right and leads to Westport Island. I remembered that if I passed the Wiscasset Information Booth I had gone too far. Sure enough, there was the sign, so I turned right and followed the blacktop road through the countryside and over the bridge. There were about six more twisty-turny miles, and then once again I saw the familiar shape that is the Squire Tarbox Inn.

I found everything literally in apple-pie order, because on that particular day there were three apple pies fresh out of the oven, and Annie McInvale invited me to have a bite with a piece of delicious cheese.

I carried the apple pie along with a glass of cold milk out to the freshly painted deck with the new wooden tables and gay umbrellas which is in a sheltered nook between two of the buildings. Elsie White pointed with pride to a screened-in gazebo decorated with pots of geraniums.

The Squire Tarbox is a very quiet inn in a section of Maine that is sufficiently off the beaten track to be unspoiled and natural. The bedrooms are very cozy in a real "upcountry" manner, and there is plenty of opportunity to sit around in front of the fireplaces in the sitting and dining rooms and enjoy conversation.

Guests can go blueberrying or raspberry picking, walk down the pine-needled path to Squam Creek, and swim or fish in Montsweag Bay, nearby.

Perhaps the real feeling at the Squire Tarbox is expressed by a letter I received from a gentleman in Cincinnati who wrote me about his experiences there during the summer of 1977:

"Elsie White and Ann McInvale are operating this inn with one thought in mind—the comfort, relaxation, and pleasure of their guests. Anne is one of those people who actually enjoys cooking! What she can do with squash, beets, zucchini, and other vegetables! We have never in all our travels had such interesting and delicious meals, and getting up in the morning was a real treat because she greeted us with fresh, homebaked blueberry muffins and homemade toasted bread.

"Our room in the barn area was clean and comfortable, and the whole atmosphere of the place made it so easy to rest and relax. I could go on, but I did want you to have a brief outline of our pleasurable stay at the Squire Tarbox Inn. After this experience we look forward to staying at other inns in your book whenever the opportunity affords it." It is true that the rooms in the barn have that

wonderful, delightful feeling that comes from years of aging and mellowing. Filled with books and photographs and reproductions of the work of Andrew Wyeth, the sitting room in the barn has a great old wood stove to take the chill off on nippy mornings. I should add that the bedrooms in the main house are, as might be expected, homey and comfortable.

Travelers passing through the Wiscasset area might be interested in having dinner at the Squire Tarbox, but let me advise a telephone call for reservations. The dining room is very small and reservations are almost always necessary.

THE SQUIRE TARBOX INN, Westport Island, R.D. #2, Box 318, Wiscasset, Me. 04578; 207-882-7693. A restored colonial home on Rte. 144 in Westport, 10 mi. from Wiscasset. European plan. 6 rooms with shared baths; two with private bath. All lodgings include continental breakfast. Breakfast served to houseguests only. Dinner served to travelers by reservation daily, except Sunday. Open from mid-May to mid-Oct. Golf, tennis, pool, sailing, exploring, walking nearby. No pets. Anne McInvale and Elsie White, Innkeepers.

Directions: From Maine Tpke. take Exit 9 follow Rtes. 95 and 1 to Rte. 144, 8 mi. north of Bath. Follow Rte. 144 to Wiscasset-Westport Bridge. Inn is located 6 mi. south of bridge on Westport Island.

THE BRADLEY INN
Pemaquid Point, New Harbor, Maine

I reached out and put my hands on the firm stone base of the Pemaquid Point Lighthouse. It radiated a wonderful warmth borrowed from the brilliant September sun, so I sat down and rested against it, attempting to draw into myself some of its strength and nobility. It was my lighthouse.

Immediately in front of me, this selfsame sun created momentary jewels where the Atlantic gently lapped against the striated rocks that stretched out toward Spain. Overhead sea birds wheeled and turned and talked to each other incessantly. I closed my eyes and my thoughts drifted back to my arrival at the Bradley Inn, which is just a short pleasant walk from my lighthouse.

Early the previous evening I had taken I-95 to coastal Route 1 and continued on through Brunswick, Bath, and Wiscasset. Following Ed Ek's directions I turned off on Business Rte. 1 at Damariscotta, turned right at the top of the hill at the white church, and followed Rte. 130 fourteen miles to Pemaquid Point and the Bradley Inn.

The first greeting came from a toy poodle who barked a welcome. This was followed with an introduction to Ed and Louine Ek and Grandma, who is a definite part of the innkeeping team. We passed underneath the blue awnings of the entranceway, through a screened-in outdoor summer dining area, into a sitting room that looked very much like what I would expect to find in a Maine farmhouse.

I paused for a moment to read the blackboard that listed the menu offerings for my Sunday night visit—prime ribs of beef, leg of lamb, veal piccata, scallops cooked in white wine, a seafood casserole, Maine lobster, and several different desserts, including the famous Bradley Inn pie, for which there is now a recipe in the *Country Inns and Back Roads Cookbook.*

The Eks and Grandma are very natural, likable people for whom the Bradley Inn has become not only a way of life, but has perhaps taken on higher meanings. Ed and Louine fled the corporate life and the environs of New Jersey to seek something with greater meaning and the opportunity to be of helpful service to more people. Louine is completely in charge of the cooking, and Ed is the host and man-of-all-work.

A visit to this country inn on the rocky coast of Maine is in many respects a step backward in time. The bedrooms all share bathrooms and conveniences "down the hall." Much of the furniture came from Ed's and Louine's former home and besides decorator sheets and pillowcases in bright colors, these moderately sized rooms have firm mattresses and colorful bedspreads.

The old-fashioned dining room provides meals not only for guests, but many people from the immediate area who consider the Bradley Inn "their inn."

While the Pemaquid Point Lighthouse is certainly one of the big attractions, both by day and by night, for this inn I found there were such other pleasures and diversions as Pemaquid beach which is the most northerly sand beach on the coast of Maine, wonderful walking in the woods and along the shore, visiting the restoration of historic Fort William Henry, a walking tour of the seaside village of New Harbor, or canoeing on the Pemaquid River.

With all of this, my lighthouse is only a four-minute walk away!

THE BRADLEY INN, Rte. 130, Pemaquid Point, New Harbor, Me. 04554; 207-677-2105. A 12-room country inn (no private baths) located near the Pemaquid Lighthouse on Maine's rocky coast, 15 mi. from Damariscotta. Many cultural, historic, recreation facilities nearby. Rooms are available year-round. Breakfast available to inn guests year-round. Open daily to the public for dinner from mid-June to mid-Oct.; on weekends only Oct. to Jan., March to June. Restaurant is closed Christmas Eve, Christmas Day, Jan., Feb. Tennis, swimming, golf, canoeing, backroading, woodland walks, xc skiing all available nearby. Edwin and Louine Ek and Grandma, Innkeepers.

Directions: From South: Maine I-95 to Brunswick/Bath coastal Rte. 1 Exit. Follow Rte. 1 through Brunswick, Bath, and Wiscasset. Exit business Rte. 1 at Damariscotta. Turn right at top of hill (white church), follow Rte. 130, 14 mi. to Pemaquid Pt. From North: Rte. 1; exit at business Rte. 1, Damariscotta. Turn left at white church onto Rte. 130. Follow 130, 14 mi. to Pemaquid Pt.

THE COUNTRY CLUB INN
Rangeley, Maine

Rangeley, Maine, is one of those places in the world that has a special kind of charisma. There are few locations that offer such beauty and grandeur in all seasons. The combination of wide skies, vast stretches of mountain woodland, and the placid aspect of Rangeley Lake have been drawing people to this part of western Maine long before the roads were as passable and numerous as they are today.

Innkeeper Bob Crory of the Country Club Inn, who is something of a phrase-maker, says, "The dramatic lake and mountain scenery surrounding us will tranquilize even the most jangled nerves."

He and I were sitting on the deck of the inn which, along with the lounge, the dining room, and many of the accommodations, enjoys a mind-boggling panoramic view.

"There's a funny thing about all of this," said Bob speculatively, "I've been a "big" hotel man all my life, but even when Sue and I were managing Sebasco Lodge we always wanted to have our own small, cozy, resort inn, and we found it here. It was built by millionaire sportsmen in the 1920s and was enlarged in recent years.

"We're planning on being a year-round operation. It's very handy to have an eighteen-hole par 70 golf course a short nine-iron shot from our front door, and it's also very convenient to have the excellent fishing for square-tailed trout and landlocked salmon in all of the Rangeley lakes that are nearby."

He excused himself for a moment and Sue Cory, who is a most attractive blonde, took his place. "I see Bob's been extolling our virtues," she said with a smile. "You know, he's so enthusiastic and we've all been so happy and our guests have been so pleased with what we've done here that it's really been a wonderful experience." She shivered a little as the sun had now gone down and suggested that we go inside for a cup of tea in front of the fireplace.

The cathedral-ceilinged living room has heavy beams, wood paneling, many, many different types of comfortable sofas, armchairs, and rocking chairs. There were several jigsaw puzzles in various states of completion, a huge shelf of books, and a great moosehead over one of the two fireplaces.

"We have lots of programs going on here, including nature slide talks, barbershop quartets, bingo, movies, sing-a-longs, astronomy slide talks, and then we go out on the terrace on a clear night and try to find the stars we've been talking about.

"We have occasional dinner dances and theme parties such as luaus and Oktoberfests. We're just a short distance from Lakewood where there is one of the oldest summer theaters in Maine."

As we sat chatting for a few moments I happened to remark to Sue that I was looking for a phrase that might possibly best describe the furnishings and decor of the Country Club Inn.

"That's easy," said Bob, taking in everything in one grand gesture of his arm. "We're posh-rustic!"

THE COUNTRY CLUB INN, Rangeley, Maine 04970; 207-864-3831. A 25-room resort-inn on Rangeley Lake in Maine's beautiful western mountain-lakes country, 45 mi. from Farmington. European, modified American plans. Open mid-May to mid-Oct. Breakfast, lunch, dinner served to travelers. Near many cultural, historic, and recreational attractions. Swimming pool and lake swimming, horseshoes, bocci, and 18-hole golf course on grounds. Fishing, saddle horses, water skiing, canoeing, tennis nearby. Bob and Sue Crory, Innkeepers.

Directions: From Maine Tpke.: take Auburn Exit 12 and follow Rte. 4 to Rangeley. From Vt. and N.H.: take I-91 to St. Johnsbury; east on Rte. 2 to Gorham, and Rte. 16 north to Rangeley.

CHARMWOODS
On Long Lake, Naples, Maine

Charmwoods is a unique type of inn. Set in an area of great natural beauty and maintained by conscientious hosts, the inn provides a perfect setting for an escape to the countryside.

Once a private lakefront estate, Charmwoods radiates all the flavor and ambience of the Maine woods but is a mere 2½-hour drive from downtown Boston.

As hosts, Marilyn and Bill Lewis make for a perfect combination. Marilyn is attractive and vivacious, and delights in giving her guests personal attention so as to ensure them the most pleasurable of vacations.

Bill, a former editor at the *Boston Globe* and *Boston Herald,* has unusual interests which Charmwoods guests find to be a pleasant diversion. For example, he often entertains with his 1890 Thomas A. Edison phonograph, drawing from a collection of about 500 cylindrical recordings—some of them predating the turn of the

century. Also among his collectibles are vintage telephones and an ancient apple corer and peeler.

Marilyn's penchant for decorating is particularly evident in all the spacious bedrooms with their selection of handsome coordinated sheets, blankets, towels, and other accessories in distinctive colors. The master suite boasts a sunken Roman-style bathtub. Every suite enjoys a view of the lake.

The focus of activity at Charmwoods is frequently the commodious and gracious living room with its massive fieldstone fireplace and panoramic view of lake and mountains. Everything about this room encourages friendly discussions with a free exchange of information and ideas. The striking undersea photographs are provided by the Lewis's son, Jonathan.

Within fifteen minutes after my arrival Bill and Marilyn had introduced me to their guests and we were immediately on a first-name basis—chatting as would old friends. Several guests were regulars at Charmwoods, having returned for second or third visits. Some were planning another stay during foliage time in the fall.

Adjoining the living room and sharing center stage during much of the year is a broad deck with an unobstructed view of Long Lake. It is equally ideal for sunny breakfasts or for chatting under the stars.

A path leads down a few steps to the shoreline of this delightfully clear lake where a powerboat, rowboat, and canoe are docked in the boathouse. Swimming from the white sandy beach or private sundeck is ideal, and a trim cabana provides numerous amenities, including telephone service.

The village of Naples, a short stroll down the road, offers guests some interesting upcountry diversions, not the least of which is a seaplane flight providing an excellent overview of the entire resort area. The *Songo River Queen,* an old-fashioned paddleboat, and the U.S. Mailboats run excursion trips across this ten-mile lake. There is plenty of backroading and quite a few antique shops in the immediate area.

During my visit at Charmwoods nearly all the guests clutched tennis rackets, and the all-weather court saw plenty of play. There's a lakeside golf course and riding stables just a few minutes away.

Visiting Charmwoods is like being a guest at a houseparty for friends.

CHARMWOODS, Naples, Me. 04055; 207-693-6798 (off season 617-469-9673). Four bedrooms, all with private baths, plus guest cottage. Located on the west shore of Long Lake, approx. ½ hr. from Main Tpke. Open from May 30 weekend into Oct. Breakfast is the only meal served (to houseguests only). Tennis, swimming, boating, canoeing, shuffleboard, and horseshoes on grounds; horseback riding, golf, and para-sailing nearby. Summer playhouse just down the road. Not suitable for children under 12. No pets. No credit cards. Marilyn and Bill Lewis, Innkeepers.

Directions: From Boston: follow Rte. 1 north to I-95 to Exit 8 (Portland-Westbrook). Turn right and follow Riverside St. 1 mi. to Rte. 302. Turn left (west) to Naples. Charmwoods is just beyond the village on the right with an unobtrusive sign. From North Conway, N.H.: follow Rte. 302 through Bridgton. Charmwoods sign and driveway off Rte. 302 just west of Naples village.

HARTWELL HOUSE
Ogunquit, Maine

The story of my first visit to this inn begins with a sumptuous lunch at the Whistling Oyster overlooking Perkins Cove in Ogunquit. I was lamenting to John Parella that we seemed to have gone back to "square one" as far as being able to recommend an accommodation in Ogunquit.

Many years ago when I first included the Whistling Oyster, John recommended that I visit the Island House, which at that time was located just a few steps beyond the "Oyster," and for many years the combination worked very well. Then, unfortunately the Island House went out of business, and again we were faced with the original problem.

"Wait a minute!" he exclaimed, "I think I have just the place for you to see. It's called the Hartwell House, run by Trisha and Jim

Hartwell, and it's a beautiful, elegant, sophisticated small inn, actually within walking distance of where we are right now."

My first glimpse of the Hartwell House on the Shore Road leading back to the center of Ogunquit was most favorable. It was a two-story pleasantly designed building fronted with many Moorish arches. There were some gardens in the front and what appeared to be some considerable grassy acreage to the rear.

The unusually large, and attractively decorated front porch area had beautiful summer furniture with lighthearted slipcovers. There were several groups of comfortable chairs and sofas, stacks of books and magazines, and many varieties of flowers. Four houseguests were playing bridge. It had the kind of atmosphere that invited me to sit down and feel at home.

Trisha Hartwell suggested that this would be a good time for us to see the accommodations at Hartwell House since many of the guests were having dinner at the Whistling Oyster, so I embarked on a rather happy journey through a group of attractively furnished rooms, some with four-poster beds, with many antiques and beautiful bedspreads. The rooms in the back of the inn also had balconies overlooking the rear lawn.

"We're planning on making some conservative additions, including tennis courts and a gazebo," explained Trisha. "Nothing that will interfere with the very pleasant country house atmosphere. I imagine it will be a couple of years before it's all completed. Our lawn leads down to the river and our guests presently enjoy sitting quietly under the trees."

There are nine accommodations at Hartwell House including two efficiency apartments and two studios. All have private baths. These have full-sized kitchens, if the guests desire. At present there are no meals offered because Trisha is very enthusiastic about some of the nearby restaurants that serve delicious breakfasts.

Hartwell House is within walking distance of the beach, Perkins Cove, churches, and the Marginal Way. It's also on the minibus route that serves the town.

So once again I'm happy to be able to recommend lodging accommodations in Ogunquit in keeping with the elegance and tone of the Whistling Oyster, which does not have lodgings but serves both lunch and dinner. I'm certain that our readers will find the Hartwell House a very pleasant experience.

HARTWELL HOUSE, 116 Shore Road, Ogunquit, Maine 03907; 207-646-7210. A 9-room inn providing a very compatible atmosphere for a limited number of guests (4 rooms may be rented as a complete apartment). No meals offered. Open April to Nov. The ocean, Perkins Cove, the Marginal Way, Ogunquit Playhouse all within walking distance. Fishing, golf, swimming, bicycles, sailing, nearby. Shared tennis and swimming pool privileges. Not suitable for children under 14. No pets. Trisha and Jim Hartwell, Innkeepers.

Directions: Follow I-95 north through New Hampshire into Maine; take last exit before Maine toll booth; north on Rte. 1, 7 mi. to center of Ogunquit. Turn right on Shore Road approx. ¾ of mi. Hartwell House on right.

THE PENTAGOET INN
Castine, Maine

"Have another bran muffin," said Natalie Saunders, with a somewhat steely look in her eye. "I've been up making them since six o'clock this morning." Actually I need no urging to take another of these delectable creations made hot and fresh every morning.

I was having a summer breakfast on the outside porch of the Pentagoet Inn looking right down the street to the harbor area where one of the romantic Windjammer sailing vessels had been moored for the night. "Some of the passengers stayed with us last night," said Natalie, buttering another of her own muffins. "You see, Castine is a regular stop on the cruise and sometimes they come in to take a shower, and they stay for dinner, too."

The Pentagoet Inn is a gracious Victorian lady with a rather interesting past, and I must say that its present and future under Natalie's watchful eye is very bright.

My lodging room had a washbowl, and a shared bath—in fact, there were two of them within just a few steps of the door. The rather austere white walls were relieved by some colorful prints. The double bed had a comfortable mattress, and there was an old-fashioned table with a lamp beside it. A chest of drawers, a com-

fortable chair, and two braided rugs completed the furnishings. Other bedrooms were similarly furnished, and all of them had a wealth of books, magazines, and fresh flowers in season.

Guests at the Pentagoet are drawn together by two factors. First, there's a very friendly arrangement of comfortable furniture in the living room, which is an extension of the dining room. Classical music is usually playing in the background on the stereo, and it's the kind of a room that encourages conversation.

The second factor is the innkeeper, who has a wonderful knack for sensing those of her guests who would prefer to be alone and those who would enjoy meeting and talking to other guests. Her own range of interests is wide enough to make everybody feel much at home. Place cards are used to assign seating at the tables. Since there's limited space in the dining room, and many people travel in twos, it's necessary to introduce two couples who may be sharing a table for four.

Natalie spoke most appreciatively of the inventiveness of her chef. "We serve a five-course, single-entrée, fixed-price dinner and the menu is published each week in the *Castine Patriot,* the weekly newspaper. Incidentally, dinner is preceded by a Pentagoet 'happy hour' each afternoon and seems a very civilized way for inn guests to get acquainted. I've noticed that it's the beginning of many fast friendships."

A very attractive woman crossed the village street in front of the inn. "Oh, I want you to meet Jean de Raat," said Natalie enthusiastically. "She's the proprietor of The Water Witch, a nifty little shop that designs and makes fine clothing from exotic, imported fabrics. As a matter of fact, she designed and made this dress that I have on this morning, a batiked cotton from the Dutch East Indies."

THE PENTAGOET INN, Castine, Maine 04421; 207-326-8616. A 14-room inn in a seacoast village on the Penobscot Peninsula, 36 mi. from Bangor. Some rooms with shared baths. Breakfast and dinner served to travelers. Dinners are single entrée prix-fixe. Tennis, swimming, backroading, village strolling nearby. Clean, leashed pets permitted. Natalie Saunders, Innkeeper.

Directions: From south follow I-95 to Brunswick and use Rte. 1 exit. Follow Rte. 1 to a point 3 mi. past Bucksport. Turn right on Rte. 175 to Rte. 166 to Castine.

GREY ROCK INN
Northeast Harbor, Maine

"I just love honeymooners!" Janet Millet was moving deftly about in the living room at Grey Rock, laying places for the continental breakfast. The snowy napery was a fitting complement to the elegant breakfast china, and I was struck by the fact that the sitting room had now, indeed, become a bright breakfast room with a view through the trees of some of the boats on Northeast Harbor.

Carefully placing the plates, fresh breakfast rolls and breads, she continued, "I just love it when honeymooners call up to make reservations, and when possible we try to put them into the Tree House where we have a minimum stay of four nights. I think it's ideal for honeymoon couples. For one thing it is a few steps away from the main house here at Grey Rock, and it's a very cozy, rustic cottage with beamed ceilings and a Franklin stove which is sometimes used in late spring and fall. There is a small kitchen over there as well, and maybe the new bride can practice a little before starting in earnest." This last was said with a slight smile.

"Many of our honeymooners in the past years have come back for anniversaries. I find that they invariably prefer the more elegant atmosphere here in the main house."

"Elegant" is an excellent word to describe Grey Rock and almost immediately new arrivals are struck with Janet's unusual collection of wicker pieces which are rare art forms. For example, there is a tea table on wheels, a chaise lounge, three or four wicker table lamps, a wicker floor lamp, wicker love seats, a wicker desk, a wicker plant stand for two plants, and wing-backed chairs in wicker. These are all in the main sitting room and another smaller adjacent parlor.

These wicker pieces blend beautifully with the unusual collection of oriental memorabilia that Janet has gathered over the years, making this house somewhat reminiscent of a New England house of a century ago when sea captains brought back the wonderful treasure of the Orient on their clipper ships. Particularly impressive are the collection of fans and the exquisite framed oriental paintings on silk. As part of the harmonious whole, fresh flowers complete the picture.

Many beautiful and informative books with full-color illustrations on things both British and American are piled on the coffee table and again contribute to this wonderful "at home" feeling. Janet, as I have said many times, originally came from England and she brings with her the innate sophistication that comes from someone who has lived for many years among beautiful things.

Although the Tree House is certainly an ideal honeymoon hideaway, all of the lodging rooms at Grey Rock have a very romantic atmosphere. A special care has been taken by Janet to furnish them with harmonizing quilts and curtains. The beds are even turned down at night!

Grey Rock literally sits on a rocky ledge above the remainder of the town of Northeast Harbor well within its own forested area where trails lead into the woods. There is no amusement or recreation on the grounds for smaller children. The entire kaleidoscope of the wonderful natural attractions of Mt. Desert Island are literally at the front door.

GREY ROCK INN, Harborside Rd., Northeast Harbor, Me. 04662; 207-276-9360. A 12-room village inn in the town of Northeast Harbor, Me., adjacent to Acadia National Park and all of the attractions of this unusual region. European plan. Continental breakfast served to houseguests only. No other meals served. Small cottage available for minimum 4-night stay. Season from early spring to Nov. 1. Children 14 yrs. and older preferred. No pets. No credit cards. Janet Millet, Innkeeper.

Directions: Located on the right-hand side of Rte. 198 approaching the town of Northeast Harbor. Note sign for inn. Do not try to make a right-hand turn at this point, but proceed about one block, turn around and approach the inn on the left up the steep hill.

THE OLD FORT INN
Kennebunkport, Maine

Shana Aldrich and I were seated by The Old Fort Inn swimming pool on a warm August afternoon. I must say she looked very fetching in her bathing suit. We were discussing how it felt to live in a place where it is like being on a vacation much of the time.

"Oh, I like it very much," she said. "I can play tennis, go swimming, and go to the beach. I always have a good suntan." Shana will be five years old in 1982.

Meanwhile, we were joined by her father David, who is the innkeeper along with her mother. "I see that you've been getting the first-class treatment from our hostess," he said with a twinkle in his eye. "She's one of our greatest assets."

The Old Fort Inn is a very special kind of country inn. The main building of a hotel that had been on the property at one time was torn down and the handsome stone carriage house was converted into twelve efficiency apartments that include daily maid service and an enclosed garage. These apartments are attractively decorated with harmonizing draperies, slipcovers, and furnishings and all have fully-equipped kitchen facilities. The rooms are large enough that guests can stay for longer periods without feeling cramped. They have electric heat. Guests gather at the lodge, located in a converted barn built around 1880. It has a big fireplace that serves as a meeting point on spring and fall evenings, and its open deck next to the swimming pool makes it a very comfortable place for guests to gather in the warmer weather. The furnishings complement this handsome, rustic room with its huge beams and weathered pine wallboards. The antique shop has also been enlarged.

David took up where Shana left off, "We've done a number of things since your last visit. Our guests really appreciate the washer and dryer that is now available. We've also installed a TV in all the rooms because we have many guests who come here for long stays and we found that they were bringing their own sets.

We were joined at poolside by Sheila who came with large welcome pitchers of real lemonade. Two of the guests at the inn strolled by on the way to the tennis courts speaking French. "We've always had a great many visitors from Canada," Sheila commented. "We're not too far from Montreal or Quebec City and there are times here during the summer when French is heard as frequently as English."

Our conversation turned to the fact that it is so very pleasant here in Kennebunkport during May or October. "I'm so glad that we installed a cover on our heated swimming pool, so now it's possible to swim earlier and later in both seasons. Fall and spring are the times when it is wonderfully quiet. As you know, midsummer in Kennebunkport is rather hectic."

We all went over to the lodge and Sheila spoke enthusiastically about the generous continental breakfasts. "It's a wonderful social time for guests," she said. "They can meet, chat, and make plans. We have orange juice, plenty of excellent coffee and a variety of homemade breads."

The inn has a very warm clublike atmosphere and is located in the residental section of Kennebunkport just a short walk from the beach. There are two golf courses nearby plus lots of boating, fishing, and ocean swimming in season. There is an excellent summer theater just a few miles away.

Although many of the guests prepare their own meals in the fully equipped kitchens or on individual outdoor barbecues, David and Sheila are happy to provide a complete rundown of all the area restaurants. "Of course we think very highly of the Whistling Oyster in Ogunquit. During the warm weather there are usually dozens of fascinating restaurants and we usually try to keep up-to-date on all of them."

OLD FORT INN, Old Fort Ave., Kennebunkport, Me. 04046; 207-967-5353. A 12-apartment resort-inn on Cape Arundel within walking distance of the ocean in a historic Maine town. Includes a continental breakfast, and a full kitchen is provided with each apartment. Daily maid service. Balconied club room. Open from May 1 to Oct. 31. Heated pool, tennis court, shuffleboard on grounds. Bicycles, golf, salt water swimming and boating nearby. Not comfortable for children under 7. No pets. Sheila and David Aldrich, Innkeepers.

Directions: Use Exit #3 (Kennebunk) from Maine Tpke. Turn left on Rte. 35 to Kennebunkport and follow signs to inn.

WHAT IS INNKEEPING REALLY LIKE?

"During the winter and early spring we managed to get a lot of clearing done in the woods, and our eventual goal is to have walking paths and benches and quiet areas for guests. Indoors, we began work on the second floor. We stripped and refinished the hall woodwork and wallpapered the hall. New carpeting was installed on the stairways and through the second and third-floor halls. Three of the seven bedrooms on the second floor have new carpeting; the carpeting for the other four rooms is here and waiting for a time of emptiness when we can have it all installed. We have the wallpaper for one room that will be our next project. We have picked out the papers for the other rooms and just need lots of time and a little money. The rooms will each be different with old-fashioned prints. We have dressed the windows with white wide ruffled Country Curtains and have made a start toward white old-fashioned spreads for the beds. I have just completed a knitted afghan for one of the double beds and we hope to have handmade quilts or afghans for all of them. We opened four rooms on the third floor for the summer, and have been using them through October. Due to lack of insulation, we must turn off the water to the third floor shortly, and probably won't be able to use it again till April. There is a slight possibility that we could have two more rooms available on the third floor, but my guess now is that we will continue to operate with eleven rooms and use the other two for live-in help in the summer."—Maine

"Each succeeding year we have made large improvements and in spite of bad economic conditions, high interest rates, cost of gas, etc., we have exceeded our wildest expectations of financial success. Your advice two years ago to postpone any major spending until after the third full year of operation was great advice. The wait didn't hurt us and we feel it actually helped not to have additional money pressures.

The vignettes 'what is innkeeping really like' are excellent — some joy as well as tears, but excellent reading for novice as well as pro. Keep these up and try to expand them even more. I almost fell off my chair when I read mine but am proud as punch and still feel exactly the same!" — Virginia

"Well, the reality of being an innkeeper certainly did set in with those last two storms! It turned out that your visit on Saturday a.m. wasn't just as the electricity was able to be restored. Our next task in the dark and quiet house was to find and invent ways of keeping cold five days' worth of dairy products, produce, and two big freezersfull. Not easy as the hours became days with no electricity. By Sunday afternoon a tall cypress tree by the cottage snapped at the base and hung posed over a guest's lovely new Porsche!! So it had to be taken down rather than let go of its own accord." — California

Continued on page 114

I do not include lodging rates in the descriptions, for the very nature of an inn means that there are lodgings of various sizes, with and without baths, in and out of season, and with plain and fancy decoration. Travelers should call ahead and inquire about the availability and rates of the many different types of rooms.

"European Plan" means that rates for rooms and meals are separate. "American Plan" means that meals are included in the cost of the room. "Modified American Plan" means that breakfast and dinner are included in the cost of the room. The rates at some inns include a continental breakfast with the lodging.

New Hampshire

WOODBOUND INN
Jaffrey, New Hampshire

Even after more than seventeen years of writing about country inns, I'll have to admit that it's always a thrill to get an *overseas* telephone call for further information about inns in any of our *Country Inns and Back Roads* series. This time there was a telephone call from Venezuela, and the man on the other end of the line (he sounded as close as the next town) said that he had a large family and wanted to stay for a few weeks at a place where everybody could enjoy themselves both with indoor and outdoor recreation and where there were other families with children.

He said they were interested in diversions such as swimming, sailing, canoeing, boating, and fishing and that he and his wife also enjoyed golf and tennis. "We've never taken a vacation in the United States before," he said, "and I realize that this is a pretty unusual request, but we wanted a place that would be 'peculiarly American.'"

After a few more questions, I narrowed the choice down to the Woodbound Inn which seemed to just about fill the bill for our South American neighbor. All of the recreation he mentioned was available plus a great many more things, including handcraft workshops, square dances, cookouts, beach lunches, along with such indoor recreation as ping-pong, pool, shuffleboard, electronic games, and even a music machine.

In addition to the Woodbound's 1,200-yard par 3 golf course with nine holes, there are four full-length 18- and 9-hole golf courses nearby. As far as fishing is concerned, there is a half-acre trout pond developed in a natural setting, and Lake Contoocook has wide-mouth bass, perch, and pickerel.

The Woodbound especially welcomes families and has cottage units that are designed particularly for them with maid service and meals at the inn. There are regular programs and activities for children and a baby-sitting service as well.

When I told the gentleman from Venezuela all of this and about how I had enjoyed my stays at Woodbound over the years he felt that this would be just perfect for his purposes.

Well I'm glad to say that the story has a happy ending. They were able to book rooms at Woodbound and, in fact, had such a marvelous time that they are planning to come back in 1982!

Families can also enjoy winter sports here, including downhill and cross-country skiing on the grounds, ice skating, tobogganing, and even snowshoeing.

The very colorful brochure of the Woodbound has a picture of the entire family — Ed and Peg Brummer (mother and father) and Jed and Mary Ellen and their three children. Jed's sister Martha has also joined the staff. Sanderson Sloane Brummer was born on July 15th, so now there is one more potential innkeeper. With so much going on I guess they need all the help they can get!

WOODBOUND INN and COTTAGES, Jaffrey, N.H. 03452; 603-532-8341. A 44-room resort-inn on Lake Contoocook, 2 mi. in the woods from West Rindge or Jaffrey. Within walking distance of Cathedral of the Pines. Both American and Mod. American plan available. Overnight European plan available in spring and late fall. Special rates for retirees in June and fall. Breakfast, lunch, and dinner served daily. Open all four seasons. Par 3 golf course, swimming, beach, sailing, water skiing, tennis, hiking, children's programs, downhill ski area, 22 miles of groomed ski-touring trails, tobogganing and lighted skating rink. Ed and Peggy Brummer, Jed and Mary Ellen Brummer, Innkeepers.

Directions: From Boston, follow Rte. 2, then Rte. 119 to Rindge where there are directional signs to inn. From New York, follow I-91 to Bernardston, Mass. Proceed on Rte. 10 to Winchester, then Rte. 119 to Rindge and watch for signs to inn.

THE DANA PLACE INN
Jackson, New Hampshire

Betty Jennings and I were standing in the middle of her garden and she was explaining that the entire output is used on the menu at the inn. "Well, there is the squash, the tomatoes, the parsley, lettuce, the carrots," she said, "and then we have a few herbs which are increasing in number every year."

We continued our walk through the grounds along the Ellis River, and she explained how the cross-country ski trails can also be used for walking during the summertime. The path led around the great boulders, through an orchard and came out at a pool formed by a natural basin in the river. "This is where we cross over in the winter," she said, "If it is too icy, there is a little trolley on a cable and you can pull yourself across the river to get to the other side. It is possible to ski from here right on down into Jackson, and a great many of our guests do it. Also, the people from Jackson come up for our lunches. It is just the right kind of a distance."

It was early September and I dipped my hand into the pool and found the water was still warm. I was tempted to dive off the rocks at the deep part. It looked so clear and inviting.

Earlier in the summer, I had talked with Chris Jennings who was working at the Black Point Inn on the Maine coast. He graduates from Bates in June '82. His sister Page will enter college that fall; both have grown up working at the inn.

The Dana Place is a historic inn. There has been an inn here since the late 1800s. At one time it was a farm, as is evidenced by the many apple trees. Like so many New England dwellings, it has been through additions, with buildings snuggled up against each other. Now its L-shape has many comfortable, homey bedrooms of different sizes and shapes.

The location within the White Mountain National Forest offers opportunities for mountain climbing, hiking, walking, and has some access to alpine trails above the timber line for the avid and experienced climber. The lower mountains invite those who prefer easier walking and enjoy the pleasure of beautiful woodland paths and cross-country skiing. Guests can order picnic lunches for walks or drives through the countryside or into the mountains.

Betty and I continued our stroll and talked for a moment about the food. "We think of ourselves as sort of country gourmet," she said. "For example, this summer we had a cold peach soup on the menu which was very popular. Our veal and ham in a casserole, and veal sauteed with butter, fresh mushrooms, wine and artichokes was also very well received. We also serve chicken Gloria which is chicken sauteed in butter with brandy and apricots. I do all the desserts, including a cranberry torte pie which is just wonderful. I also do the cheesecake and French chocolate custard served with whipped cream. By the way, we make hot mulled cider from our own apples."

By this time we had completed our big circle next to the river, through the woods and open fields and were walking toward the inn with its white clapboard buildings. The green mountains provided a contrasting background.

Betty sighed contentedly and said, "It is really beautiful here most of the year. I love the summers and fall, but to me there is nothing like seeing all this covered with snow and having lots of cross-country skiers gathering together at night around the fireplace. I am so glad we are innkeepers."

DANA PLACE INN, Route 16, Pinkham Notch, P.O. Box 157-B, Jackson, N.H. 03846; 603-383-6822. A 15-room resort inn, 5 miles from Jackson, N.H. in the heart of the White Mountains. Rates include lodging and full breakfast. Lunches served on winter weekends only. Dinners served to travelers daily from late May to late Oct. and from mid-Dec. to late April. Closed Thanksgiving Day. Two tennis courts, natural pool, trout fishing, xc skiing, birdwatching, on grounds. Hiking trails, indoor tennis, 5 golf courses, downhill skiing nearby. Malcolm and Betty Jennings, Innkeepers.

Directions: From Rte. 16, north of Jackson Village toward Pinkham Notch. The Dana Place is a flag stop for the Trailways through bus to and from Boston.

THE DARBY FIELD INN
Conway, New Hampshire

"Norm, this is the place where the cross-country ski trails go up the mountains and into the woods. I designed the course and cut most of the trails myself."

It was about ten o'clock in the evening, but fortunately the light of the full moon enabled me to see the course taken by these trails. The late July night was filled with the scents of a mountaintop in New Hampshire, and the butternut, birch, maple, and blue spruce trees created ghostly shadows and shapes under the bright moon.

My guide for this after-dinner walk was a young man I've come to know rather well in the last 25 years or so. I can certainly attest to his abilities as a designer of trails, because he has made several near our farmhouse in the Berkshires. I'm also indebted to him for some excellent cross-country ski instruction. He is my younger son Keith Simpson, who now makes his home in Tamworth, New Hampshire.

In the company of Marc and Marily Donaldson, innkeepers of the Darby Field Inn, we had enjoyed a most pleasant dinner by candlelight in the warm precincts of the dining room with its truly spectacular view of the surrounding forest and mountains. Marc has had experience working in country-inn kitchens, including the Three Mountain Inn in Vermont, as was evidenced by the menu which included several veal dishes and chicken Marquis. I enjoyed the filet mignon with a very delicious mushroom sauce. The maple chiffon pie which we enjoyed immensely was also one of his concoctions.

Our impromptu reunion began in the living room, which is divided into two areas with one side taken up by a huge stone fireplace and a hearth which extends to the end of the stone wall. The large black andirons were substantial enough to hold even the heaviest of logs during the winter season. The fireplace was further distinguished by shelves with plants, cranberry glass, and candles.

Adjacent was the lounge with a sizable Franklin stove on a brick hearth, pine paneling, and tweedy, comfortable chairs. The bentwood chairs around the small oak tables had black leather cushioned seats. I was very pleased to see so many plants scattered about the inn and lots of books and magazines. The sophisticated rustic feeling was further carried out by French Impressionist posters. The lounge looks out on a grassy slope with a rock garden of nasturtiums, geraniums, marigolds, and ferns.

Marc and Marily Donaldson are two of the youngest of *CIBR* innkeepers, even though they have three children, the eldest of which is a very active six-year-old, Jeremiah. "I think he has the makings of an innkeeper," said Marc proudly.

"What we've had in mind all along is a pleasant informal place where people of all ages can come and enjoy themselves in all four of our seasons and get the real feel of the White Mountains." Marc continued, "Marily and I have had a great time going around to yard sales and antique shops, buying quilts, knicknacks and the like to make the rooms more homey and bright."

Nine of the eleven rooms at the Darby Field have private baths and are furnished with country-inn furniture, featuring lots of calicoes and checks. Most have a splendid view.

The swimming pool area is bordered by boulders and sur-rounded by woodlands with ferns, day lilies, spruces and birches. Amusing touches are the fish fountain at one end of the pool, and the sculptured squirrels clambering up the pole-lamps at the corners of the pool area.

Keith and I continued our walk and he remarked enthusiasti-cally that the inn is in the Mount Washington Valley where there's golf, fishing, theater, and a number of other recreational attractions nearby. "There are five mountains with downhill skiing here," he said, "and you can see for yourself that cross-country skiing starts right at the front door."

Of course, this winter I've got to go back and visit the warm, comfortable Darby Field Inn, have dinner again with Marc and Marily, and try those cross-country ski trails myself.

THE DARBY FIELD INN, Bald Hill, Conway, N.H. 03818; 603-447-2181. An 11-room White Mountain country inn, 3 mi. from Conway, N.H., within convenient driving distance of all of the Mount Washington Valley cultural, natural, and historic attractions, as well as several internationally-known ski areas. Modified Amer-ican plan. Open April 30 to Oct. 30; Thanksgiving weekend; Dec. 17 to Mar. 28. B&B only Thanksgiving to Dec. 17. Swimming pool and carefully groomed cross-country skiing trails on grounds. Tennis and other sports nearby. Marc and Marily Donaldson, Innkeepers.

Directions: From Rte. 16: Traveling north turn left at sign for the inn (½ mi. before the town of Conway) onto Bald Hill Rd., and proceed up the hill 1 mi. to the next sign for the inn and turn right. The inn is 1 mi. down the dirt road on the left.

DEXTER'S INN AND TENNIS CLUB
Sunapee, New Hampshire

"Tennis is one of our middle names, and so is cross-country skiing in the winter." Shirley Simpson and I were enjoying a walking tour of Dexter's Inn, when she stopped for a moment to return an errant tennis ball that came rolling across the lawn after one of the guests had hit an overhead smash that bounded over the fence. "Our tennis courts are all-weather so we can play as early in the spring as possible and even on warmish days in November and December.

"We have cross-country skiing on 12½ miles of trails. These are used for walking in the summer and fall. You should really come during the last week of September. The leaves are already turning and it is the best time to be in New Hampshire. It's not crowded at all."

We walked past the swimming pool and into the cool deep woods for a few yards and came out at a lovely little chapel. "This was built some years ago," she said. "Many of our guests enjoy this walk—it is so quiet and peaceful, and it is a good place for bird-watching, or for picking the wildflowers in the fields."

"A big event this year was the wedding of our daughter Holly. She announced that she wanted to be married at the inn in September. It was a beautiful wedding, the weather cooperated and we had 136 guests outside. There was a bower of flowers in front of our willow tree, contra dancing on the lawn, and a delicious table on the terrace. It was really the prettiest wedding and we're going to bring pictures to the annual *CIBR* meeting in Florida."

The lodging rooms at Dexter's Inn are fun. The accent is on very bright and gay colors, in wallpaper and curtains and bedspreads. The rooms in the main house are reached by using funny little hallways that zig-zag around the various wings.

The front parlor has a baby grand piano, a lovely old antique desk with copies of newspapers and magazines, a very inviting fireplace, and lots of books.

There are other bedrooms with a rustic flavor located in barns across the street. These barns also have a recreation room which is keyed for young people who need a place of their own. There is ping-pong, bumper pool, a television set, and just about every indoor game that has ever been invented.

The menu includes sauerbraten, fresh sole amandine, Chinese-style pork and vegetables, and breast of chicken done in wine and mushrooms. Cooks also do apple crisps and blueberry buckles, and bake homemade bread every day.

Dexter's is a resort-inn and there is something for almost everybody to enjoy. Many guests stay for quite a few days and even a couple of weeks at a time. One guest in particular, Norman Arluck, a gentleman of some 73 years, has visited many times and plays a wicked game of tennis and also many different types of card games. He's really a whiz.

In a letter I received this year from Norman, he said, "I'm flattered that you included me in *CIBR;* however, in the interest of accuracy, I must point out to you that I am in my 77th year. I've been at Dexter's since June 25th and hope that I'll see you this year, and if not, at least during 1982."

Norman, I wouldn't miss it.

DEXTER'S INN AND TENNIS CLUB, Box R, Stagecoach Rd., Sunapee, N.H. 03782; 603-763-5571. A 17-room country inn in the western New Hampshire mountain and lake district. Mod. American plan; European plan available in June and Sept..only. Breakfast, lunch, and dinner served to travelers by advance reservation; closed for lunch and dinner on Tues. during July and Aug. Lunches served only July, Aug.; Dec., Feb. Open from early June to mid-October. Open on a limited basis from late Dec. through mid-March. Suggest a phone call well in advance. Closed Thanksgiving and Christmas Day. Pets allowed in Annex only. Limited activities for children under 12. Three tennis courts, pool, croquet, shuffle-board, 12½ mi. of xc skiing on grounds. Downhill skiing and additional xc skiing nearby. No credit cards. Frank and Shirley Simpson, Innkeepers.

Directions: From North & East: use Exit 12 or 12A, I-89. Continue west on Rte. 11, 6 mi.-just ½ mi. past Sunapee to a sign at Winn Hill Rd. Turn left up hill and after 1 mi., bear right on Stagecoach Rd. From west: use Exit 8, I-91, follow Rte. 103 east into N.H.-through Newport ½ mi. past Junction with Rte. 11. Look for sign at "Young Hill Rd." and go 1½ mi. to Stagecoach Rd.

ROCKHOUSE MOUNTAIN FARM
Eaton Center, New Hampshire

Rockhouse Mountain Farm really has a great story. It is a family-run farm-inn that for thirty years has been a way of life for John and Libby Edge, and their now-grown son, Johnny, and daughter, Betsi who is married to Bill Ela.

It is not only family-run, but definitely oriented for family vacations. Just imagine taking young children to a place where there are riding horses, cows, ducks, geese, chickens, pigs, piglets, ponies, pheasants, guinea hens—all with their own names!

What about the chance to help with farm chores like haying, milking, and grooming the horses? How about the opportunity to learn not only how to canoe, but where the best blueberries are located on Foss Mountain. Think of a barn filled with hay, with swings and tunnels, and chances for playing hide-and-seek on rainy days.

There are also sailboats, rowboats, and canoes at the Rockhouse private beach, located on Crystal Lake. Then think about fresh rolls or bread every day, fresh vegetables, special desserts, and all that anyone can eat, prepared daily by Betsi.

After I had seen the lodging rooms, dining rooms, parlors and the 200-year-old barn and met all of the animals, including the eighteen little ducklings (eighteen? a new record!) belonging to Pearl, the Muscovy duck, and also a few of the twenty little piglets belonging to Buttercup and Sweetpea, Johnny's prized sows, and surveyed the beautiful vegetable garden, Johnny summed up the spirit of RMF this way, "We have tried to create an inn for families because we believe the family was the basis of society, business, and religion in colonial times, and should be the basis of our life today. Families that can vacation together and spend leisure hours together have a chance to grow together and understand one another.

"We have tried to make available to our guests the simple way of life. They can enjoy things like running through the fields and chasing our dogs, cantering along a country road as the sun rises over the hills or sliding down the waterfalls of Swift River.

"I think Dad and Mother have always seen in our place the opportunity for a 'refresher' period—a chance to exchange everyday concerns over coffee at breakfast, to enjoy the quietness of dinner by candlelight, and to exercise the body with things like tennis and golf.

"You would have to stay with us for at least a year to see all there is to do in this part of New Hampshire, and to do all there is to do at Rockhouse."

Libby Edge reminded me of the pleasant tradition that has been going on for some years at the inn. "When our first guest departed thirty years ago one of us grabbed an old school bell and rang it as a farewell. We have been doing it ever since. One bell has grown to a variety of nine, and all the guests join the Edges lined up on the front driveway as the cars of guests roll away from Rockhouse. It has gathered more sentiment as the years have gone by and everyone anticipates the royal sendoff."

RMF is informal, rustic, and gregarious. The happiest guests are those willing to lend a hand with the chores, "do" the dozens of White Mountains things together, and sit around the table talking long after it has been cleared. Long may it prosper.

ROCKHOUSE MOUNTAIN FARM INN, Eaton Center, N.H. 03832; 603-447-2880. A complete resort in the foothills of the White Mountains (6 mi. south of Conway), combining a modern 18-room country inn with life on a 350-acre farm. Some rooms with private bath. Mod. American plan. Open from June 15th through October. Own saddle horses, milk cows, and other farm animals; haying, hiking, shuffleboard; private beach on Crystal Lake with swimming, rowboats, sailboats, and canoes—canoe trips planned; stream and lake fishing; tennis and golf nearby. No credit cards. The Edge Family, Innkeepers.

Directions: From I-93, take Exit 23 to Rte. 104 to Meredith. Take Rte. 25 to Rte. 16, and proceed north to Conway. Follow Rte. 153, 6 mi. south from Conway to Eaton Center.

HICKORY STICK FARM
Laconia, New Hampshire

I carefully separated the first bite of my first breast of roast duckling at Hickory Stick Farm, and prepared to transfer it to my expectant mouth. I could plainly see the succulent textures and colors. The outside was crisp and beautifully browned, and the meat underneath the skin was moist with just enough juice. I placed the tender morsel in my mouth and was immediately transported.

I take a lot of ribbing among the many innkeepers of my acquaintance for having a penchant for roast duckling. I've eaten it everywhere, from Longfellow's Wayside Inn in South Sudbury, Massachusetts, on New Year's Eve, to the Inn at Rancho Santa Fe, California. Now, I was in the Shangri-la of the world of roast duckling, the place where other roast duckling specialists want to go when they have roasted their last duckling—Hickory Stick Farm in Laconia, New Hampshire.

It's located on the top of a hill outside of Laconia, (see directions below) in a very busy section of the resort area of New Hampshire, dominated by Lake Winnipesaukee.

The entrance to this old converted farmhouse is through a lovely old-fashioned door leading into a beamed, low-ceilinged room with a brick fireplace which, at the time I was there, had some antiques on display. The floors are of brick or stone and there are antiques and gift items scattered about in several rooms which precede the entrance to the restaurant itself. The stenciling on some of the walls was done by Mary Roeder and is after the manner of Moses Eaton, Jr., who used to travel around southern New Hampshire in the early 1800s as a journeyman stencil artist. I believe some of his original work is in the Hancock Inn in Hancock, New Hampshire.

Mary and Scott Roeder (his brother Steve is at the Dockside Restaurant in York, Maine) showed me to a table with a most pleasant view of the fields, woods, and valleys with Mount Kearsage, Ragged Mountain, and Cartigan in the distance. (Scott explained that a man with a chain saw has to whittle away at the trees in order to keep the view of the mountains.) Outside, the lilac and forsythia bushes were augumented by maple, butternut, apple, and locust trees, and I noticed several birds fluttering about in the branches.

Besides the duckling, the menu had many other items on it such as veal a la Hickory Stick, seafood, and steaks, but it was to the duckling section that my eye was immediately drawn. I could have ordered a quarter of a roast stuffed duckling, a half, or a whole one for two, three, or four persons. They are all served with a country herb dressing and orange sherry sauce. Scott asserted that at least 75 percent of all of his entrées served are for roast duckling.

As the duckling on my plate disappeared, Scott went on to elaborate on the message that can be found on each table about how the ducklings are cooked. "This process involves roasting at a low temperature for about eight hours, which extracts about a pound of grease from each bird," he explained. "The ducks are then refrigerated, and as orders are received from the dining room, they are placed in a very hot oven for fifteen to twenty minutes. This final roasting

extracts even more grease and produces a duckling which is golden brown.

In a recent letter Scott advised me that he is no longer shipping individual orders for duckling. He writes, "Nowadays, shipments of frozen ducks are delivered by refrigerated trucks to Pfaelzer Brothers in Chicago who then ships them anywhere in the country, and there are about sixty stores in New England that carry Hickory Stick Farm roast ducklings."

HICKORY STICK FARM, R.F.D. #2, Laconia, N.H. 03246; 603-524-3333. A hilltop country restaurant (no lodgings available) 4 mi. from Laconia in the lake country of New Hampshire. The Shaker Village in Canterbury is nearby, as well as the Belknap recreational area and other New Hampshire attractions. Open from Memorial Day to Columbus Day. Dinners served from 5:30 to 9 p.m. Sunday dinner served all day from noon to 8 p.m. Extended hours during fall foliage season—call ahead. Scott and Mary Roeder, Innkeepers.

Directions: Use Exit 20 from I-93. Follow Rte. 3 toward Laconia approximately 5 mi. over bridge over Lake Winnisquam. A short distance past this bridge on the right is a drive-in restaurant (Double Decker), turn right on Union Road immediately past Double Decker and follow Hickory Stick signs 1½ mi. into the woods. If you do not turn onto any dirt roads, you are on the right track. From Laconia go south on 3 & 11 (do not take 106) and turn left on Union Road (about ½ mile past the Belknap Mall) and follow signs.

PHILBROOK FARM INN
Shelburne, New Hampshire

Once again zooming across Route 2 in western Maine, I caught a glimpse of the three main houses of the Philbrook Farm Inn tucked away underneath the mountains on the north side. The warm sun of late September caught the sparkle of many early turning leaves as well as the white clapboards of the house. I remember this was almost the same time and the same sensation I had had a few years ago when I first turned off the road to discover what for many people is a truly unusual New Hampshire country inn experience.

The Philbrook Farm Inn *is* New Hampshire. There is New Hampshire to be seen everywhere: New Hampshire prints, paintings, and photographs—some of them really irreplaceable. There are tints of old prints, hooked rugs, and many, many books about New Hampshire, in fact a whole library of books on the White Mountains alone. Some have been written by former guests.

Once again I followed the road over the railroad crossing and then traversed the rumbling planks of the single-lane bridge over the river. I followed the road and pulled up underneath the old apple trees in front of the inn and hoped that I would be in time to have at least a bowl of soup or some dessert from the Sunday lunch.

The garden was at its most gorgeous peak; I've never seen the flowers in more impressive bloom and the cornfield across the road had silken tassels. This is certainly one of the most gentle and pleasant times to visit the Philbrook Farm Inn, but there are other seasons, too.

Wintertime is waking up in the morning to snowstorms, and brilliant sunshine, seeing white-capped Mt. Washington over the hills in the distance, and also looking at the cross-country ski wax thermometer which gives advice on the correct wax for the day. The fields, which in summertime have Herefords standing knee-deep in the lush grass, are filled with snow.

The wealth of outdoor activity in all seasons encourages the kind of appetites that most people never knew they had. Consequently, food is on everybody's mind at least three times a day. "It is all homemade with no mixes," said Connie Leger, the innkeeper, along with her sister Nancy. "There is one main dish each night, and the dinner usually consists of a homemade soup, some type of pot roast, pork roast, or roast lamb. The vegetables are all fresh and we try to stay away from fried foods. Most of the guests enjoy roasts, because these days they are not served as much at home. All of the desserts are homemade. There's pie, ice cream, and pudding.

"For lunches, we serve salads, chowder, hot rolls, hash, macaroni and cheese, and things like that. Breakfast is a real big farm-style breakfast. On Sunday morning we have New England fish balls and cornbread."

Besides farmhouse lodgings in the three main buildings, some of which have private baths, in the summertime guests enjoy several different cottages, some with housekeeping arrangements and their own fireplace. These too enjoy a view of the meadows, river, and the mountains beyond.

During my visit this time, I had a long talk with a lady from Boston who has been coming to the farm since 1937. She told me that her husband first came here in the early 1900s when it took six days to get here from Cambridge, Massachusetts. "He's been coming almost every year since," she said. "I think we are the oldest living graduates."

Well, I missed the lunch, but was honored to be invited to sit in the kitchen with Maxine and Tilly and enjoy a bowl of good chicken soup near the ten-burner woodburning range which was built before the turn of the century. As Nancy pointed out, "We do almost all of our cooking and baking on this range, and only use the electric stove in case of emergency."

PHILBROOK FARM INN, North Rd., Shelburne, N.H. 03581; 603-466-3831. A 20-room country inn in the White Mountains of northeastern N.H., 6 mi. from Gorham and just west of the Maine/N.H. line. American, mod. American, and European plans available. Open May 1 to Oct. 31; Dec. 26 to April 1. Closed Thanksgiving, Christmas. Shuffleboard, horseshoes, badminton, ping-pong, croquet, pool, hiking trails, xc skiing, snowshoeing trails on grounds. Swimming, golf, hiking, backroading, bird watching nearby. Pets allowed only during summer season in cottages. No credit cards. Nancy C. Philbrook and Constance P. Leger, Innkeepers.

Directions: The inn is just off U.S. Rte. 2 in Shelburne. Look for inn direction sign and turn at North Rd., cross R.R. tracks and river, turn right at crossroad, and the inn is at the end of road.

LOVETT'S BY LAFAYETTE BROOK
Franconia, New Hampshire

It was a warm Sunday afternoon in July and some of the guests at Lovett's were swimming in the natural brook across the country road from the inn. The maple tree, one of the first to turn to its fall colors in this section of the country, was providing cool green shade for guests engaged in animated conversation.

Lovett's is a sophisticated country inn with a spectacular view of Cannon Mountain with its many ski trails. There is considerable emphasis on excellent food and service, and the inn is well into its second generation of one-family ownership.

The main house of Lovett's actually dates back to 1790. It was built by Nicolas Powers, the original homesteader, and he was one of the petitioners to the state asking for aid to build a road through Franconia Notch.

Many of the guests have been returning for years, their fathers and mothers having come before them. "It is," one guest remarked, "almost like a club."

Summer in Franconia has many delights—antiquing, horse shows, summer theater, flower shows, auctions, and country fairs. Most of the ski areas run their lifts during the summer and autumn. Shopping seems to intrigue Lovett's guests, and there is a sprinkling of country stores and craft shops throughout the mountains.

Still another of the interesting side trips for Lovett's guests is a visit to the Robert Frost Museum which is not more than a ten-minute drive away. It can be identified by the legend, "R. Frost" on the mailbox.

On the campuslike grounds of the inn there are poolside chalets and others with mountain views and living rooms, many of them with fireplaces. These are furnished in bright contemporary fashion and are preferred by guests who enjoy the idea of being at the inn, but not so much a part of it. There are also several traditional country inn bedrooms in the main house and in two nearby houses.

Of the two swimming pools, one has rather chilly mountain water that comes right off nearby Cannon Mountain, and the other has a solar heater; one of the first in the area, I am sure.

With Lovett's impressive reputation for its food, it is difficult to make a choice from the tempting menu.

When I pressed Charlie Lovett to tell me which dish was most favored, he had this to say, "We're particularly proud of our cold bisque of native watercress, our eggplant caviar, and our pan-broiled chicken in brandy, herbs, and cream. People also tell us they enjoy our braised sirloin of beef Beaujolais, and lamb served with our own chutney."

While I sat with Charlie in the sheltered ell overlooking the solar heated pool, he told me the good news about the New England Ski Museum which is to be established in Franconia Notch next to the tramway, "where it all began," he said.

"It is for all the New England states and will contain much memorabilia and history of some of the great early Austrian ski instructors, such as Hans Schneider, who really provided the impetus that eventually resulted in the American ski industry. We were in on the early part of everything around 1930 and had our own Swiss ski instructor here. He took the guests up on Cannon Mountain every day. In those days you herringboned up the side of the mountain because there was no ski lift as there is now."

LOVETT'S BY LAFAYETTE BROOK, Profile Rd., Franconia, N.H. 03580; 603-823-7761. A 32-room country inn in New Hampshire's White Mountains. Modified American plan omits lunch, although box lunches are available. Breakfast and dinner served by reservation to travelers. Open daily between June 29 and Oct. 8 and Dec. 26 and April 1. Two swimming pools, xc skiing, badminton, lawn sports on grounds. Golf, tennis, alpine skiing, trout fishing, hiking nearby. No pets. Mr. and Mrs. Charles J. Lovett, Jr., Innkeepers.

Directions: 2½ mi. south of Franconia on N.H. 18 business loop, at junction of N.H. 141 and I-93 South Franconia exit. 2¾ mi. north of junction of U.S. 3 and 18.

COLBY HILL INN
Henniker, New Hampshire

The comfortable chair by the wood stove which had been installed in the big fireplace was so inviting that I picked up the guests' register at the Colby Hill Inn and settled down to browse through some of the comments. Guest registers are fun. Most of the time there are happy, and sometimes witty and bright, comments from enthusiastic guests.

Don Glover, Sr., came down the stairs and through the living room, noticing what I was reading. "It's interesting how many people pick up the guest register, just the way you have. It makes fun reading, don't you think so?"

Don and his wife June were classmates of mine at Bucknell University, and a few years ago they, along with their son, Don, Jr., and his wife, Margaret, acquired this classic New Hampshire inn from former owner Bettie Gilbert.

The inn is on the outskirts of the small village of Henniker which, among other things, is the home of New England College. The ceilings are low, the walls are hung with oil paintings and prints, and the furnishings are country antiques. A grandfather clock ticks away in one corner. There are birds during all seasons and a gorgeous flower garden during spring and summer. In earlier times, the living room fireplace was used for baking bread.

Lodging rooms at the inn are typical country New England. Many have candlewick bedspreads, hooked rugs, old bowl-and-pitcher sets, which are reminiscent of the days when water was brought in from the outside. Some of them have shared bathrooms and all of them have that wonderful, old "home" feeling.

"This is great cross-country skiing terrain," said Don. "There are forty miles of trails in this vicinity and a great many of our guests, including the children, come up for long weekends or even, when possible, during the week."

At that moment I caught the aroma of freshly baked bread coming from the kitchen, so Don and I wandered back to where Don, Jr., was getting things ready for dinner. Don, Jr., and I had a short conversation about the expanding menu. "We serve chicken Colby House," he said, "and this, along with our fresh seafood, has been received very well. We have specials almost every day and usually a fresh fish of the day. My mother has her own little baking corner here and she does the chocolate cakes, the cinnamon buns, the biscuits, and the applesauce. We have a lot of things on the menu that have grown in our garden, including juice from our own tomatoes. She also made some jelly from wild grapes that grow out behind the barn."

One of my favorite things at this inn is a delightful swimming pool sheltered by an ell formed by the two huge barns adjacent to the inn. It is most welcome on hot days of the southern New Hampshire summer.

This inn is enjoyable in many seasons because this section of New Hampshire has many lakes, state parks, golf courses, summer theaters, and antique shops which add to the attraction for vacationers or weekenders.

COLBY HILL INN, Henniker, N.H. 03242; 603-428-3281. A 10-room inn on the outskirts of a New Hampshire college town. European plan. Some rooms with shared baths. Breakfast served to houseguests only. Dinner served to travelers Tuesdays through Sunday, except Thanksgiving, Christmas, and New Year's Day. Open year-round. Swimming pool on grounds. Tennis and xc skiing one short block; alpine, 3 mi.; golf, canoeing, hiking, bicycling, and fishing nearby. No children under 6. No pets. The Glover Family, Innkeepers.

Directions: From I-89, take Exit 5 and follow Rte. 202 to Henniker. From I-91, take Exit 3 and follow Rte. 9 through Keene and Hillsborough to Henniker. At the Oaks, W. Main St., one-half mile west of town center.

THE INN AT CROTCHED MOUNTAIN
Francestown, New Hampshire

The first thing that comes to mind when I think of this inn is the fabulous view.

One of the intriguing things about this view, which can be enjoyed from a great many lodging rooms as well as from the dining

room, living room, the terrace, and the swimming pool, is that it gets better with each visit.

When I mentioned this to Rose Perry, she laughed merrily and said, "Oh, we think so, too. Even though John and I have been looking at this view for many years, it becomes more and more meaningful to us."

There were many other most intriguing aspects besides the fabulous view with which this very attractive Indonesian-Chinese woman acquainted me. Rose's father is a hotelier in Singapore, and she lived a number of years in Hong Kong. Rose and John met while attending Paul Smith College, which is a hotel school in the Adirondacks. In complete charge of the kitchen, she does most of the cooking, and I was surprised at the unusual number of main dishes, many of which are her own recipes.

I first visited Crotched Mountain early in June when the late New England spring is at its most delicious with apple blossoms and lilacs, and I was smitten by the wonderful panorama stretching out for miles.

On September 25th, the time of my second visit, the fall colors were magnificent as only they can be in the Monadnock region, where occasionally the full range is reached before October first.

It was during this visit that I enjoyed a leisurely dinner and had the opportunity to see John and Rose Perry and the inn in a different light. There was a glowing fire in the low-ceilinged parlor of the little pub where after-dinner guests and other couples dropped in during the evening.

My lodging room had a fireplace, and windows overlooking the mountains and valleys; also a door through which I could step directly outside to the swimming pool.

The next morning I took a few moments to wander around on the broad green lawn and look out over the valleys. "It looks this way in Indonesia," Rose said, as she joined me for a few minutes. "It's just like the mountains and valleys in Djakarta. The floating mist on the mountains has an Indonesian look."

As I walked toward the car, John remarked that this was a different world in the winter when Crotched Mountain skiers would be walking the short path to the lift line, and the cross-country skiers would be headed into the woods.

The views are many at the Inn at Crotched Mountain.

THE INN AT CROTCHED MOUNTAIN, Mountain Rd., Francestown, N.H. 03043; 603-588-6840. A 14-room mountain inn (4 rooms with private baths) in southern New Hampshire 15 mi. from Peterborough. Within a short distance of the Sharon Arts Center, American Stage Festival, Peterborough Players, Crotched Mtn. ski areas. European plan. Open from Memorial Day to Oct. 31; from Thanksgiving to the end of the ski season. Breakfast, lunch, and dinner available to travelers in summer; breakfast or dinner, during winter and fall (telephone for reservations and exact schedule). Closed Easter. Swimming pool, tennis courts, volleyball on grounds. Golf, skiing, hill walking, and backroading in the gorgeous Monadnock region nearby. No credit cards. Rose and John Perry, Innkeepers.

Directions: From Boston: follow Rte. 3 north to 101A to Milford. Then Rte. 13 to New Boston and Rte. 136 to Francestown. Follow Rte. 47 2½ mi. and turn left on Mountain Road. Inn is 1 mi. on right. From New York/Hartford: I-91 north to Rte. 10 at Northfield to Keene, N.H. Follow 101 east to Peterborough, Rte. 202 north to Bennington, Rte. 47 to Mountain Rd. (approx. 4½ mi.); turn right on Mountain Rd. Inn is 1 mi. on right.

SPALDING INN CLUB
Whitefield, New Hampshire

Many years ago the White Mountains in New Hampshire had numerous summer resorts where "mother and children" might come up early in the season and where "father" joined them for the last four weeks or so. These resorts were wonderful, gay places where everything that was needed for a long complete vacation was either on the grounds or nearby. The lure of the mountains drew people in great numbers from Boston and New York.

Now, with few exceptions, all of these family-run resorts have disappeared, but not the Spalding Inn Club which is thriving under second and third-generation owners and innkeepers. Many of the amenities of earlier times are still preserved. For example, gentlemen

wouldn't think of going into dinner without a jacket and tie, and the inn is a focal point for the sports of lawn bowling and tennis, with several tournaments scheduled from mid-June to mid-September including the U.S. National Singles and Doubles Lawn Bowling Championships.

The Spalding Inn Club is an excellent example of entertainment and hospitality that can be provided for a family with many different preferences. For example, on the inn grounds there are four clay tennis courts, a swimming pool, a nine-hole par-3 golf course, two championship lawn bowling greens, and shuffleboard. Five golf courses are within fifteen minutes of the inn and plenty of trout fishing and boating, and enticing back roads are nearby. The Appalachian Trail system for mountain climbing is a short walk from the inn.

There is also a well-blended balance of vigorous outdoor activity and quiet times including an extensive library, a card room, and a challenging collection of jigsaw puzzles. Groves of maples, birches, and oak trees native to northern New Hampshire are on the inn grounds and there are over 400 acres of lawns, gardens and orchards.

There are real country inn touches everywhere. The broad porch is ideal for rocking, and the main living room has a fireplace with a low ceiling, lots of books and magazines, baskets of apples, a barometer for tomorrow's weather, a jar of sour balls, and great arrangements of flowers.

Those country-inn touches also include the traditional hearty menu items so satisfying after a day of outdoor activities in the White Mountains. Among other offerings are delicious clam chowder, oyster stew, boiled scrod, poached salmon, pork chops, roast duckling, roast tenderloin, and sweetbreads. Children love the Indian pudding. All of the pies, including hot mince, the breads, and rolls are made in the bakery of the inn.

An innovation at the inn includes completely furnished and equipped cottages that are available for rental periods of three days or longer from December to April. This makes winter activities including downhill and excellent cross-country skiing, as well as snowmobiling and snowshoeing, available during the New Hampshire winter.

I am just as pleased and proud as I can be that Ted and Topsy Spalding continue to keep their standards high and that this delightful, elegant, resort-inn continues to offer its unique White Mountain hospitality.

SPALDING INN CLUB, Mountain View Road, Whitefield, N.H. 03598; 603-837-2572. A 70-room resort-inn in the center of New Hampshire's White Mountains. American plan only from late May to mid-October when breakfast, lunch, and dinner are served daily to travelers. Housekeeping cottages only from mid-December to April. Heated pool, tennis courts, 9-hole par-3 golf course, 18-hole putting green, two championship lawn bowling greens, and shuffleboard on grounds. Also guest privileges at 5 nearby golf clubs. Trout fishing, boating, summer theater, and backroading nearby. Ted and Topsy Spalding, Innkeepers.

Directions: From New York take Merritt Pkwy. to I-91; I-91 to Wells River, Vt. Woodsville, N.H. exit; then Rte. 302 to Littleton, then Rte. 116 thru Whitefield to Mtn. View Rd. intersection—3 miles north of village. From Boston take I-93 north thru Franconia Notch to Littleton exit; then Rte. 116 thru Whitefield to Mtn. View Rd. intersection—3 miles north of village. From Montreal take Auto Route 10 to Magog; then Auto Route 55 and I-91 to St. Johnsbury, Vt.; then Rte. 18 to Littleton, N.H. and Rte. 116 as above. The inn is situated 1 mi. west on Mountain View Rd.

STAFFORD'S IN THE FIELD
Chocorua, New Hampshire

The first sight that caught my eye was the family of ducks. Two good-sized adults and at least ten baby ducklings were waddling their way across the parking lot down toward the new tennis court which was in its final stages of construction. I tried as unobtrusively as possible to get a closer view of the duck family, but they would

have none of it, and kept moving farther away into the high grass with mama and papa duck carefully herding the little ones out of harm's way.

The muted tan colors of the main building had a fresh look, with the gay accents of window boxes and a summer garden of black-eyed Susans and other seasonal flowers. The big old red barn, which I have admired since my first visit in 1971, was still intact and I'm sure was being put to some intriguing uses this summer.

Next to the kitchen door a small table, shaded by a bright blue umbrella, had a sign saying, "Bakery." Another small sign indicated that cookies, sandwiches, and other things would be available for guests for noontime forays into the countryside. I found Ramona Stafford and had a nice chat with her while she was doing the morning muffins. On the wooden table were the necessities and trappings of baking: a large bowl of eggs, a blender, a box of oats, a brush with melted butter, five or six recipe books, and on the shelf all kinds of tempting flavorings, in addition to a contraption for weighing and measuring the ingredients.

In the 1972 edition of *Country Inns and Back Roads* I pointed out that this was an inn of many faces. It sits at the end of the road at the top of a small hill with broad meadows on three sides and a beautiful woods behind. There is an apple orchard, stone walls, a series of small cottages, and that famous barn. A great many of the winter guests are fond of cross-country skiing and there are trails all around the inn.

Still another face of this old inn is seen in summer when the New Hampshire mountains offer many diversions including water sports like canoeing, sailing, fishing, and swimming. It's possible to find a place of unusual peace and contentment by disappearing into the woods surrounding the inn. For the more vigorous climber, Mt. Chocorua offers a worthy challenge.

Today, as in 1972, still another side of Stafford's in the Field is Ramona's gourmet cooking. I hasten to point out that "gourmet" is a word I never use lightly, but my original conversation with her convinced me that she was not merely a good cook but a dedicated searcher for true expression in the culinary art. Breads and pastries are home-baked and there is a very generous selection of Russian, French, Italian, and German dishes with a knowledgeable use of herbs and spices. One of my favorite dishes is the spare ribs cooked in maple syrup.

I joined Fred Stafford at breakfast where the houseguests were seated around the long tables, and many of them it seems were traveling with *Country Inns and Back Roads.* Some of them had used the European book to visit Europe, and one couple particularly mentioned having visited the Falsled Kro in Denmark.

Having watched Ramona turning out those muffins, my mouth was watering for them. I can report that I ate three hot from the oven and deliciously buttered; with the fourth I tried something new: cutting it up in several slices and pouring some delicious hot maple syrup over it.

Mmmm, terrific!

STAFFORD'S IN THE FIELD, Chocorua, N.H. 03817; 603-323-7766. An 8-room resort-inn with 5 cottages, 17 mi. south of North Conway. Modified American plan at inn omits lunch. European plan in cottages. Some rooms in inn with shared baths. Meals served to guests only. Closed Apr. and May, Nov. and Dec. Bicycles, square dancing, tennis, and xc skiing on the grounds. Golf, swimming, hiking, riding, tennis, and fishing nearby. No pets. The Stafford Family, Innkeepers.

Directions: Follow N.H. Rte. 16 north to Chocorua Village, then turn left onto Rte. 113 and travel 1 mi. west to inn. Or, from Rte. 93 take Exit 23 and travel east on Rtes. 104 and 25 to Rte. 16. Proceed north on Rte. 16 to Chocorua Village, turn left onto Rte. 113 and travel 1 mi. west to inn.

LYME INN
Lyme, New Hampshire

The Lyme Inn rests at the end of a long New England common, and although the village feels quite remote it is, nonetheless, just ten miles from Hanover, New Hampshire, the home of Dartmouth College, and inn guests have the opportunity to enjoy some of the sporting and theatrical events taking place there. It is just a few

minutes from the Dartmouth skiway and there's plenty of cross-country skiing nearby.

The ten rooms with private baths and five rooms with shared baths have poster beds, hooked rugs, hand-stitched quilts, wide pine floorboards, stenciled wallpaper, wingbacked chairs, and all kinds of beautiful antiques which guests frequently become very attached to and purchase. I feel certain that children would not be comfortable because there is no entertainment particularly designed for them.

The spacious front entranceway of the inn, which is used as a summer porch, has one of the most impressive collections of white wicker furniture I have ever seen, possibly equaled by the wicker at Grey Rock Inn at Northeast Harbor, Maine.

I timed my most recent visit so that I could arrive in time to have breakfast with Innkeepers Fred and Judy Siemons, and speaking of breakfast, the inn is well known in that particular department. Besides an à la carte breakfast there are at least eight other full breakfasts with everything from cheese omelets, poached eggs, English muffins, and french toast, to a north country breakfast featuring pancakes.

The main dishes on the dinner menu include hasenpfeffer, Wiener schnitzel, rack of lamb, and hunter-style veal. (Judy's recipe for hasenpfeffer is in our *CIBR Cookbook*.)

Judy was overflowing with news about the inn. "Our third dining room now has our Garrison stove and what a difference it makes both in heat and warming up the atmosphere. We found a wonderful source of braided rag rugs and have replaced many of our older rugs and covered previously bare floors with some of the nicest braided rugs I've ever seen. We've also added quite a few Hitchcock chairs and tables to our dining rooms.

"We've installed gas fires in many of our bedrooms which gives us a fire that is safe for our lovely old building."

I asked about the three boys in the Siemons family. "Ricky is in California working part-time and in school part-time and playing lots of golf which is his first love. He hopes to make a career of it; perhaps in management of some kind. Gary has been a great help around the inn, mostly sharing the breakfast detail with Fred. It's a tossup as to who cooks the meanest eggs. He's also very busy making certain that the vehicles are all in perfect running order. He has been accepted at the East Coast Aeronautical Technical School in Massachusetts to study aviation mechanics.

Our youngest, who is no longer young, is Robbie. He's been working in logging which is a very big industry up here in New Hampshire. At present he, too, is learning a great deal about automobile mechanics. He's definitely the 'outdoors' one of the family."

I would estimate that it takes about three days to really enjoy this part of New Hampshire. The Dartmouth College Theater, the back roads, local shops, fairs, auctions, and the great emphasis on handcrafts in the area, plus the skiing, both cross-country and downhill, would encourage many guests to extend their holidays. Of particular interest would be the back roads and small villages on each side of the Connecticut River. Some of the village greens and commons have endured the decades and become classics in their own right.

As my always-interesting visit drew to a close, Fred made a point of telling me that they have a great many Canadian visitors. "It's not very far from Montreal," he said, "and many of our friends from north of the border say that we are very similar to the English and Canadian inns that they like so much."

LYME INN, on the Common, Lyme, N.H. 03768; 603-795-2222. A 15-room village inn (10 rooms with private baths), 10 mi. north of Hanover on N.H. Rte. 10. Convenient to all Dartmouth College activities, including Hopkins Center, with music, dance, drama, painting, and sculpture. European plan year-round. Breakfast and dinner served daily to travelers, except dinner on Tuesdays. Closed three weeks following Thanksgiving and three weeks in late spring. Alpine and xc skiing, fishing, hiking, canoeing, tennis, and golf nearby. No children under 8. No pets. Fred and Judy Siemons, Innkeepers.

Directions: From I-91, take Exit 14 and follow Rte. 113A east to Vermont Rte. 5. Proceed south 50 yards to a left turn, then travel 2 mi. to inn.

JOHN HANCOCK INN
Hancock, New Hampshire

One of the things I enjoy doing is browsing through copies of *Country Inns and Back Roads* that were published several years ago. For example, in 1974, writing about the John Hancock Inn I quoted innkeeper Glynn Wells who was saying, "When Pat and I talked to you a couple of years ago in Stockbridge you may remember that we said we were looking to buy a country inn that actually felt like our own home. Here in Hancock we know we found it."

My account continued, "Glynn Wells was speaking as the three of us were strolling down the main street in this southern New Hampsire village after a splendid dinner at the inn. He continued, 'What we're doing now has really became a tradition with a great many of our guests—strolling the village streets and looking at these fine old homes with picket fences and big trees. Some of them

walk to the village green past the bandstand to gaze at the graceful spire of the Congregational church. It's all part of the unwinding that many guests tell us they can do here.'

"We stopped to pass the time of day with a neighbor who was tending her flowers, and talked of the upcoming Old Home Day the following week. 'Oh, I wish you were going to be here,' Pat exclaimed. 'That's the day when former residents return. What began as a family picnic a century ago has grown to a wonderful town-wide celebration complete with parade, band concert, and all kinds of sports and fun. I've been waiting for it all year.'"

That was 1974, and since that time Glynn and Pat and their two children have not only successfully operated a country inn but have also become an integral part of this small community which is in one of the prettiest villages in the Mount Monadnock region. It's not very large but what there is of it is honest and true.

The John Hancock is a prime model for a village inn. It is the continuing center for community activity and is small enough so that villagers and visitors alike have the opportunity to get acquainted. It is New Hampshire's oldest continuously operating inn and all of the lodging rooms have been appropriately furnished. Many have double and twin canopy beds.

Over the years I've shared some of Pat Wells' letters with my readers and here is an excerpt from her most recent epistle:

"I think that the whole business of innkeeping has been an act of faith for us. Back in 1972 the realization that we were going to be somewhere else was the controlling factor that led us to Hancock. God has been good these years. We believe that with his strength and guidance we can make the inn what it richly deserves to be—a haven for others, a source of pride for the town, and a deep and rich experience for our family. It is all that, I believe, but never could be without the faith that has supported us in every kind of problem.

"We find that many guests are including the John Hancock Inn in a kind of a New England sampler. They plan a circle trip that includes Boston and its many attractions, the seacoast of Maine, the higher mountains of northern New Hampshire and then a stay in our land of picturebook villages, twisty roads among the hills, and inviting vistas that comprise the Monadnock region. Happily, many come back for longer stays after a brief taste."

Like dozens and dozens of other innkeepers in *CIBR*, Pat, Glynn, Andrew, and Susan have put their hearts and hopes into their inn, doing what innkeepers in America have been doing for well over two hundred years, providing food, lodging, and comfort for traveler and villager alike. As Pat says, "The friends we have made in our community and among the inn guests have been our greatest reward."

THE JOHN HANCOCK INN, Hancock, N.H. 03449; 603-525-3318. A 10-room village inn on Rtes. 123 and 137, 9 mi. north of Peterborough. In the middle of the Monadnock region of southern N.H. European plan. Breakfast, lunch, and dinner served daily to travelers. Closed Christmas Day and one week in spring and fall. Bicycles available on the grounds. Antiquing, swimming, hiking, Alpine and xc skiing nearby. Glynn and Pat Wells, Innkeepers.

Directions: From Keene, take either Rte. 101 east to Dublin and Rte. 137 north to Hancock or Rte. 9 north to Rte. 123 and east to Hancock. From Nashua, take 101A and 101 to Peterborough. Proceed north on Rtes. 202 and 123 to Hancock.

Vermont

THE INN AT WEATHERSFIELD
Weathersfield, Vermont

The ancient Greeks believed that each of us is predestined to live our lives in a pattern devised by the gods. If indeed that is true, then Mary Louise and Ron Thorburn were each destined to become innkeepers, because seldom have I found two people who are well-suited, both in temperament and skill, for this honorable profession.

Fortunately for lovers of inns, The Inn at Weathersfield, as ancient a structure as "any in the land" provides them with a perfect setting for their roles. Located in the mountains of eastern Vermont, just west of the Connecticut River, the original farmhouse was built nearly two centuries ago. It was enlarged in 1796, a carriage house was added in 1830, and graceful pillars on the front porch, built by a homesick southern minister around 1900, supply the rather surprising "southern Colonial" look. The inn is set back from the highway and has eleven large guest rooms and a two-room suite all furnished with period antiques. Each room has a private bath, some have canopied beds, and most have working fireplaces. The dining room has exposed beams and a big fireplace.

Mary Louise and I were in the Keeping Room in front of a crackling fire and enjoying a mug of mulled wassail, which is cider made from locally grown and pressed apples. "Innkeeping has been all that we ever hoped for and even much more," she said, as she refilled my cup. "Furthermore, the concept is growing almost continually. For example, we always wanted to be able to do breakfasts on silver trays in the bedrooms, if our guests preferred. And I wanted to have the opportunity to present some of my really special recipes, including chicken Weathersfield and another one called fruit ambrosia. I also have smashing recipes for herb-cheese bread, baked in a flower pot! Dinner is served in the dining room which is such a wonderful place for everybody to get to know each other. Of course, Ron loves it because it's filled with our books, and he has his piano and plays almost every night. We're all definitely into music. Come let me show you."

As we walked into the dining room she continued, "We have facilities here for people to bring their own horses and carriages, and we also have guests who ride horseback down from the Kedron Valley Inn.

"One of the best bonuses has been the town of Weathersfield, because there are so many lovely people here and our guests can either walk or bike down to the town. We even have a bicycle built for two, and there is maple-sugaring, cider-pressing, a soapstone factory, a country print shop and a weekly newspaper. There are quite a few antique and craft shops, as well as Bingo at the firehouse on Friday evenings."

The reader can realize that I have only scratched the surface of all of the wonderful warmth and ambience of this cordial Vermont country inn. As I said at the beginning, it's almost as if the Thorburns and The Weathersfield Inn were destined for each other. Now there is a happy conviction of completeness.

THE INN AT WEATHERSFIELD, Route 106 (near Perkinsville), Weathersfield, Vermont 05151; 802-263-9217. A 12-room Vermont country inn located just a few miles east of I-91 and north of Springfield. European plan, with breakfast and a high English tea included in the cost of the room. Dinner also served. Closed for dinner, Sunday, Monday, and Tuesday (although also available on other evenings during the high season). Horseshoes, badminton, croquet on the lawn; sleigh riding on grounds. Also a natural amphitheater with music and theater offered during the summer. Many footpaths and back roads. Bicycles available. Berry and apple picking, golf, downhill skiing, (Ascutney and Okemo), xc skiing, horseback riding nearby. Children under 8 years old are not conveniently accommodated. No pets. Mary Louise and Ron Thorburn, Innkeepers.

Directions: If traveling north on I-91, use Exit 7 at Springfield and follow Rte. 106. Traveling south, take Exit 8 and follow Rte. 131 to

Rte. 106 and turn south. From Boston, leave I-89 and follow Rte. 103 across New Hampshire west into Vermont where it becomes Rte. 131 and then go south on Rte. 106.

BARROWS HOUSE
Dorset, Vermont

Charlie Schubert and I were taking a few minutes to stroll the grounds at the Barrows House and the first thing that he called to my attention was the beautiful new gazebo which he described as: "The talk of Dorset." I could see for myself that several guests were enjoying the beauty and serenity as we passed by.

I might add that Charlie has been promising me this gazebo for some time, so I'm glad it's a reality.

"The big project this year involved the creation of two bedrooms and a sitting room out of the attic space in what we call the Truffle House," he explained. "Marilyn has received so many compliments on the decor of these rooms that she is tempted to hang out her decorator's shingle. We've also completely renovated the Carriage House and transformed it into a really super accommodation.

"It is hard to realize that we've been here for ten years," said Charlie, "and I guess it's actually twelve since we first talked to you in Stockbridge about the possibilities of having a country inn.

"Oh, there have been some interesting times all right," he said. "I think that the winter of the gas shortage was the year that Marilyn and I really came of age as innkeepers. We had ordered a lot of cross-country equipment for the ski shop, made arrangements for the swimming pool to be dug that spring, and started renovating and adding new apartments in all the various old outbuildings we have here. Then, as we all remember vividly, the snow didn't come and the gasoline disappeared!"

All of that seemed far away today. The pool looked beautiful to me with the gaily colored umbrellas, the snack bar, and the "changing room," which was designed to look like a small country barn. The tennis players changed partners and started another set.

Charlie excused himself for a few moments to greet some arriving guests and I sat there in the early twilight enjoying the quiet and peace of this Vermont country town.

Dorset has always been a town in which I feel at home. I have been well-acquainted with it for more than thirty years. The streets are tree-shaded, the houses are traditionally late Colonial and early Victorian; there is a village green, a post office, and general store. I have played many a round of golf on the rather sporty course and

enjoyed many an evening of theater at the Dorset Playhouse. Incidentally, Charlie Schubert himself is an actor and during the winter he has appeared in quite a few plays given by the local company.

There is indeed a spirit at the Barrows House which I find so frequently among people who have left the city to take up a new life as country innkeepers. As busy as Charlie and Marilyn are in this thriving inn, they always seem to have time to stop and pass the time of day with their guests, help them plan an antiquing trip through the Green Mountains, arrange for a fourth at doubles or even accompany them out on the cross-country ski trails.

"Sometimes," Marilyn Schubert says, "this can be deceiving. It looks like the life of a country innkeeper is all fun and games. Believe me, maintaining 28 rooms in 6 houses, a ski shop, swimming pool, tennis courts, a full service dining room, and keeping up with all of our guests is a time-and-a-half job. Don't get me wrong, I'm not complaining. It is great fun, but there are lots of times that Charlie and I never even see each other during the day. But we love it and we wouldn't do anything else."

BARROWS HOUSE, Dorset, Vt. 05251; 802-867-4455. A 28-room village inn on Rte. 30, 6 mi. from Manchester, Vt. Modified American plan omits lunch. Breakfast and dinner served daily to travelers. Swimming pool, sauna, tennis courts, paddle tennis, bicycles, skiing facilities, including rental equipment and instruction on grounds. Golf, tennis, trout fishing, and Alpine skiing nearby. No credit cards. Charles and Marilyn Schubert, Innkeepers.

Directions: From Rte. 7 in Manchester, proceed 6 miles north on Rte. 30 to Dorset.

NORTH HERO HOUSE
North Hero, Vermont

One of the ways in which I keep in touch with *CIBR* innkeepers and their families is through what we call "Dear Norman" letters which they write me every fall. I have been reading the North Hero House yearly letters, handwritten in red ink on the familiar mustard-colored stationery, thinking Caroline wrote them. However, during my most recent visit last summer, while seated with the family on the grassy dock which extends out into Lake Champlain, I discovered that the author all of these years has really been Roger!

The North Hero House is maintained for twelve weeks every summer by Dr. Roger Sorg, who has a dentistry practice in Flemington, New Jersey, and his wife Caroline, along with David and Lynn, their son and daughter. Roger had spent several summers on the island as a boy and even in those early days dreamed of becoming the owner of the North Hero House.

Here's an excerpt or two from Roger's letter which provides us with a little insight: "We had a banner year with our fishing contest; the winning walleye was over eight pounds; the northern pike topped ten pounds and our smallmouth bass was four pounds. Our guests greatly enjoyed our fresh Lake Champlain fish entrées. Many of them enjoyed arriving by boat for an evening meal and some stayed overnight. Our motoring guests can make some interesting day trips to Montreal, Mt. Mansfield, the Shelburne Museum, the Shakespeare Theater in Burlington, and Ausable Chasm—all within approximately an hour. Our Annual N.H.H. July 4th fireworks celebration 'went off' as planned." Guests enjoy all types of water sports in addition to the tennis court and all manner of summertime fun nearby.

"Lynn is well into her freshman year at the University of Vermont. At first her biggest problem in the dental hygiene course was remembering that she was now working with "instruments" which she insisted upon calling "utensils" from her past years of experience as a cook at the inn.

"David also continues his hospitality major studies at U.V.M. In addition, he has worked part-time helping to open a fresh fish restaurant. He also has a part-time position with the Radisson Hotel in Burlington.

"Caroline is already making preparations for the '82 season. She has found some new recipes for the Sunday evening buffet and is planning some physical changes in the kitchen and some more plants to be used in the non-smoking greenhouse dining room. Our vegetable garden was terrific. Incidentally, lobster night has been moved from Thursdays to Fridays, so we will look for you some Friday night next summer!"

In addition to bedrooms at the main house, many have been added in what are, for the most part, original buildings that stretch along the shore of the lake.

I can truthfully say that since 1972 I've enjoyed ALL of my visits. Apparently another guest shares my feeling because Roger handed me a note a guest left for me which read in part: "I suppose it was with some trepidation that we returned to N.H.H. this summer after having spent time here last summer. One is never certain that good times can be repeated. This visit was even *better* than last year and since we found it through your book we wanted to tell you we hope to make our visits a tradition."

NORTH HERO HOUSE, Champlain Islands, North Hero, Vt. 05474; 802-372-8237. A 23-room New England resort-inn on North Hero Island in Lake Champlain, 35 mi. north of Burlington and 65 mi. south of Montreal. Modified American plan. Breakfast, lunch, and dinner served daily to travelers. Open from late June to Labor Day. Swimming, fishing, boating, waterskiing, ice house game room, sauna, bicycles, and tennis on grounds. Horseback riding and golf nearby. No pets. No credit cards. Roger and Caroline Sorg, Innkeepers.

Directions: Travel north from Burlington on I-89, take Exit 17 (Champlain Islands) and drive north on Island Rte. 2 to North Hero. From N.Y. Thruway (87 north), take Exit 39 at Plattsburg and follow signs "Ferry to Vermont." Upon leaving ferry, turn left to Rte. 2, then left again to North Hero. Inn is 15 min. from ferry dock on Rte. 2.

THE INN ON THE COMMON
Craftsbury Common, Vermont

Ever since my first visit to this inn in the summer of 1975 I've thought of it as a moveable feast. Perusing the previous copies of *CIBR*, I've discovered that Penny and Michael Schmitt have had something new and exciting to report every year. Before this year's update, let's take an overview:

The village of Craftsbury Common was founded in 1789 by Ebeneezer Crafts, who moved here from Massachusetts after the Revolutionary War. A great many of the buildings around the Common, which is an open, fenced piece of land, were built in the late 18th and 19th century and are still standing. The inn buildings were constructed in the early 1800s and are graceful examples of Federal architecture. There are antiques throughout generously combined with all the modern comforts. Each guest bedroom is individually decorated and supplied with fresh flowers or plants, extra pillows, and terry cloth bathrobes.

Penny Schmitt supervises the dinner which is served only to houseguests and sometimes includes fresh rainbow and brook trout available "only when the postmaster goes fishing." Breakfasts are quite elaborate with many types of omelets — cheese, herb, mushroom, onion, tomato, or even an "everything" omelet which is all of the above.

This would be quite enough for most inn-goers. However, in 1978 a swimming pool was added and an excellent tennis court and that was the first year of "cut throat" croquet played with imported English mallets and balls. That was also the year that the old building across the road from the inn was renovated and new bedrooms were added. The craft shop was opened in May, 1978.

Penny had news about the Craftsbury Sports Center which inaugurated a complete ski touring facility. There is a trail that goes from the front of the inn over the fields to the center, and cross-country skiing guests have a moveable feast of their own!

In 1979 the Center took on even greater dimensions with activities on nearby Lake Hosmer including a sculling camp, a running camp, a soccer camp, and provisions for kayaking and canoeing. Inn guests are invited to be spectators at various events, if not actually participating.

In 1981 more rooms were added and more antiques were acquired to add to the atmosphere.

In 1982, as incredible as it may seem, even further great leaps forward are planned. Penny's letter to me reads in part, "We're enlarging the dining room into the porch, keeping the outer arches and lattice work, and adding a wall of insulated glass. It will be lovely and not change the lines of building one bit. We are also planning to light the rose garden at night so that guests can look out and see the beauty even after dark. We will light it during the winter as well because the snow swirls wonderfully in that area.

"We're taking a room in the annex that was part of the shop and are turning it into a gorgeous bedroom with fireplace, the usual yummy quilts, and a private bath. We're adding a private bath to the huge bedroom upstairs in the annex overlooking the pool. We're taking the slate-floored room in the annex and making it into an entertainment center. Right now plans call for a television with a Betamax. There will be large braided area rugs, comfy sofas, pillows, and we look at this as a 'feet-up' sort of room."

Yes, over the years The Inn on the Common has indeed become a moveable feast, but may I hasten to add there's ample opportunity for sitting in the inn garden, watching sunsets, walking on country roads, reading books, and enjoying the peace and quiet of the Northeast Kingdom countryside.

A sidelight to this update is the fact that when I visited the Goose Cove Lodge in Maine in September I found Michael and Penny taking a few days of much-needed R&R and it was at that time I had an inkling of some of the exciting changes that I reported above. Penny's letter remarked that George and Elli were superb hosts, and she added, "We spent only four days there, but I could spend far longer, as we did not really have time to explore all of Deer Isle or any of the environs."

THE INN ON THE COMMON, *Craftsbury Common, Vt. 05827; 802-586-9619. A 15-room resort-inn in a remote Vermont town 35 mi. from Montpelier; 5 rooms with private bath, 10 sharing 5 baths. Modified American plan omits lunch. Breakfast and dinner served to houseguests only. Open mid-May to the Sunday after Columbus Day and mid-Dec. to mid-March. Attended pets allowed. Swimming, tennis, croquet, lawn bowling, xc skiing, snowshoeing, on grounds. Golf, tennis, swimming, sailing, horseback riding, canoeing, fishing, xc and downhill skiing, skating, hiking, and nature walks nearby. Michael and Penny Schmitt, Innkeepers.*

Directions: From the south take I-91 to St. Johnsbury exit. Take Rte. 2 west, to Rte. 15 west, to Hardwick. Then take Rte. 14 north for 8 mi., turn right and go three mi. up long curving hill to inn. From Canada and points north, use Exit 26 on I-91 and follow Rte. 58 W to Irasburg. Then Rte. 14 southbound 12 mi. to marked left turn, 3 mi. to inn.

THREE MOUNTAIN INN
Jamaica, Vermont

Seventeen-year-old Claire Murray who had just returned home from Vermont Academy in Saxton's River, Vermont, was escorting me through the Three Mountain Inn. I happened to pay a visit at a time when her mother Elaine and her father Charles were both away from the inn, but I couldn't have picked a better-informed guide.

After a very pleasant tour of the many attractive, real country-inn bedrooms, many with flowered wallpaper, comfortable beds, and a Vermont farmhouse feeling, we returned to the beautiful big sofa in front of the Dutch oven fireplace, and over a cup of tea she told me what it's like to move from the city to the country and have a family-owned country inn.

"We think it's just fabulous," she remarked enthusiastically. "My father is really a wonderful host, and my mother has been having a lot of fun developing new recipes and supervising in the kitchen. Sarah, my younger sister, who is nine years old—she's playing soccer with her friends this afternoon—just loves the idea of being in an inn. She says it's like having company all of the time."

Claire excused herself to answer the phone and I couldn't help but overhear her conversation about the walking trails in nearby Jamaica State Park. "Almost all of our guests go there. The trail follows the West River and it's an easy, not-too-steep, three-mile walk to the dam and then back. Or you can take a more difficult trail up the mountains to Hamilton Falls, where there is a series of three beautiful falls." Apparently, her answers filled the bill, because the caller made a reservation for three nights.

"I'm sorry that my mother isn't here now because she could tell you more about our breakfasts and dinners. I do know that we have

locally caught corncob-smoked trout and she makes all of the soups and quiches. One of my favorites is chicken paprikash and, boy, does she make great desserts and special ice creams!"

By this time I was beginning to work up an appetite and when I asked whether or not I could make dinner reservations, Claire looked very disappointed and said, "Oh, this is Wednesday and we don't serve dinner except to houseguests tonight."

I asked her what she liked most about living in a country inn. "First of all, I really enjoy this house," she said. "It was built around 1780 and I never thought that when we were living in the city we would actually have a home like this, and of course everyone loves this fireplace room and they keep 'oohing and aahing' about the wide-planked walls and floors. I guess the biggest thing for me, though, is the downhill skiing. We are within minutes of Stratton, Bromley, and Magic Mountain. But I also like the cross-country skiing and we can take off from our backyard. I never thought I would ever live in a house with a swimming pool, and we have one of those, too. Our guests can play tennis nearby and go fishing or even horseback riding."

The sequel to this visit took place a few months later when I stopped back and had a wonderful dinner at the Three Mountain Inn and had a chance to meet Charles and Elaine Murray and also Sarah. There's a third older daughter named Kelley. They are all enthusiastic outgoing people who have taken to the new world of country inn-keeping with great zest. The meal was every bit as good as Claire had promised me, and I think Charlie summed up their feelings by saying, "Elaine and I feel confident that we're on our way to making the Three Mountain Inn one of the finest small romantic country inns in Vermont."

I would agree that the Murray family is well on its way toward this pleasant objective.

THREE MOUNTAIN INN, Route 30, Jamaica, Vermont 05343; 802-874-4140. An 8-room inn located in a pleasant village in southern Vermont. Modified American plan. (Rates include breakfast and dinner.) Dinners also served to other than inn guests nightly except Wednesday. Closed April 15 to May 15; Labor Day to Sept. 15; Oct. 31 to Thanksgiving. Swimming pool on grounds. Tennis, golf, fishing, horseback riding, nature walks and hiking trails in Jamaica State Park, downhill and xc skiing, Marlboro Music Festival, Weston Playhouse, all within a short drive. No pets. No credit cards. Charles and Elaine Murray, Innkeepers.

Directions: Jamaica is located on Rte. 30 which runs across Vermont from Manchester (U.S. 7) to Brattleboro (I-91).

RABBIT HILL INN
Lower Waterford, Vermont

Rabbit Hill Inn was looking very spruce and trim during my visit at the end of July. The Vermont and American flags were flapping in the breeze and there were at least five cords of wood piled up just waiting to defy the cold weather and snow which was bound to come. There were very colorful plantings of flowers in front of the porch with it's gleaming Doric pillars, along with two old sleighs and an old wagon, also laden with flowers.

Across the country road in front of the inn was the famous, much-photographed church built in 1859, and the 150-year-old post office that is also an "honor system" library. In the distance the peaks of New Hampshire's famous Presidential range could be seen in the clear northern Vermont air.

"Good morning and welcome to Rabbit Hill Inn!" This warm greeting was expressed by Beryl Charlton. She and her husband Eric are the innkeepers at Rabbit Hill. "Do I detect a bit of Albion in your speech?" I asked. "Indeed you do, I'm from Stratford-on-Avon and Eric hails from Newcastle-on-Tyne, although we've lived in America for some time."

Thus began a very pleasant visit with this attractive couple and members of their family who I'm told are in residence at various times of the year depending upon their academic availability. "We all had to agree on this project at the start," explained Eric, "and even though we had two in college and one seeking a position, it's necessary for everybody to participate when possible during very busy times."

At least six of us squeezed into a small screened-in porch in the rear of the inn looking out over a spacious lawn with round tables under gay umbrellas and swings for the children. During the conversation we watched a phoebe build a nest under the eaves preparing to raise what Eric said was a second family that summer. "She's under the modified American plan," he said, his eyes twinkling.

I had plenty of time that day to wander about the inn and enjoy my room, which had access to the second-floor balcony and its own fireplace, as well as a chance to see the other twenty bedrooms, some in a more modern wing, all of which have their own private baths. "All but two of our rooms have a view of the mountains," said Beryl.

The Charltons are great collectors of antiques of all kinds, so all of the bedrooms are generously furnished with the results of their search. My room had an old Victor windup phonograph with a collection of records that included "On The Five-Fifteen," done by Byron Collins, and "I'll Take You Home Again, Kathleen," sung by Henry Burr. There was also an interesting collection of coal miners' lamps which originally came from England. Several of the bedrooms had lace-trimmed canopied beds, and the wallpapers and decorations were bright and gay, very much in the country inn theme.

A word or two about the dinner menu is in order; there are some excellent soups and appetizers including a cold salad of cucumber, orange, raisins, almonds, and yogurt spiced with a curried dressing. Entrées include mushroom goulash which is a sauté of mushrooms, green peppers, tomatoes, and onions flavored with paprika; and steak Farci which is a pan-broiled sirloin steak stuffed with mushrooms, bacon, shallots, and gruyere cheese served in a red wine sauce.

Dinner is served in the candlelit dining room which also overlooks the great mountains of New Hampshire.

Rabbit Hill is one of several inns in *CIBR* kept by British innkeepers.

RABBIT HILL INN, Pucker St., Lower Waterford, Vt. 05848; 802-748-5168. A 20-room country inn with a view of mountains on Rte. 18, 10 mi. from St. Johnsbury, Vt. Modified American, European plans. Open all year except for 2 weeks in April and November. Breakfast and dinner served to travelers. Fishing, xc skiing on grounds. Tennis, swimming, walking, Alpine skiing, sailing, backroading nearby. The Charlton Family, Innkeepers.

Directions: From I-91: Exit 20 east through St. Johnsbury, follow Rte. 2 east and signs to Rte. 18. From I-93: Exit Rte. 18 junction, turn north (left) on Rte. 18.

THE VILLAGE INN
Landgrove, Vermont

"There isn't a paved road in Landgrove." Jay and Kathy Snyder were showing me around the Village Inn in Landgrove, and as we were walking around the outside of the old inn with its red clapboards, I had remarked about the beautiful dirt road which runs directly in front. "Yes," continued Kathy, "Vermont is one of the few states that's doing its best to preserve its country roads rather than pave every single one of them. This section of the state has quite a few."

The Village Inn has been owned and operated by the Snyders for 20 years. It first opened its doors as an inn in 1939 and for many years the main interest was skiing. However, in recent years the Snyders have made it an all-season resort-inn, which is particularly attractive to families with children of all ages.

During my visit there were many active young people around, most of them in the Rafter Room which has a big fireplace, log beams across the low ceiling, and plenty of games like ping-pong, skittles, and bumper pool.

In the winter the outdoor-minded guests can enjoy downhill skiing at five major areas nearby, plus cross-country skiing, snow-shoeing, and sledding in the woods right behind the inn. There is also an ice skating pond.

Summertime activities on the grounds include tennis courts, a nine-hole pitch-and-putt golf course,. a heated pool, hiking trails, volleyball, and fishing. There is a wealth of Vermont fun nearby including horseback riding, indoor tennis, summer theatre, the Alpine slide at Bromley, hiking, auctions, music festivals, country fairs, barn dances, and church suppers.

If I seem to be emphasizing activities which may appeal to young people, it's because it's a joy to find a place where families can simply relax and enjoy good times together.

At the time of my first visit in 1976 Jay's and Kathy's daughters were quite young. Now, Kim is in the eighth grade and Heidi is in the sixth and both of them are active outdoor people—I think that's one of the reasons why other young people find the Village Inn so enjoyable.

Jay was telling me about the whirlpool spa. "It is most welcomed by our winter guests in particular," he said. "When their muscles are tired from skiing or hiking they love the relaxed feeling after being in the spa. I hope that your readers will remember to pack their swimming suits in the winter months."

Guest rooms at the Village Inn span a wide variety of tastes. Because the inn is family-oriented there are several rooms that would be adaptable for whole families, as well as bunk rooms for children. There are also rooms which are furnished in a more contemporary style. Lodgings include a hearty breakfast.

At dinner, the dining room was buzzing with people who had been having a good time all day long. Dinner consisted of a loaf of homemade bread right out of the oven, a salad with an interesting house dressing, a baked potato, green peas, and slices of rare roast beef. The strawberry shortcake was made the old-fashioned way.

And, there are no paved roads in Landgrove, Vermont. Isn't it wonderful!

THE VILLAGE INN, Landgrove, Vt. 05148; 802-824-6673. A 21-room rustic resort-inn in the mountains of central Vermont, approximately 4½ mi. from Weston and Londonderry. Lodgings include breakfast. Breakfast and dinner served to travelers by reservation during the summer except Wed. dinner. Open from

Nov. 23 to April 15; July 1 to Oct. 17. Swimming, tennis, volleyball, pitch-and-putt, xc skiing, fishing on grounds. Downhill skiing, riding, indoor tennis, paddle tennis, antiquing, backroading, Alpine slide, golf, summer theatre nearby. Children most welcome. No pets. Jay and Kathy Snyder, Innkeepers.

Directions: Coming north on I-91 take Exit 2 at Brattleboro, follow Rte. 30 to Rte. 11 and turn right. Turn left off Rte. 11 at signs for Village Inn. Bear left in village of Peru. Coming north on Rte. 7 turn east at Manchester on Rte. 11 to Peru. Turn left at signs for Village Inn. Bear left in village of Peru.

BLUEBERRY HILL
Goshen, Vermont

I first visited Tony and Martha Clark at Blueberry Hill in midsummer of 1972, when the idea of opening up an inn exclusively for cross-country skiers was just taking shape in their minds. I followed up with a mid-December trip that same year, and already a great deal of progress had been made.

In the 1973 edition, I wrote of that visit: "Here in the beautiful Green Mountains of Vermont, cross-country skiing is just about everything. On the day of my visit, it was cold; I mean *really* cold. Nevertheless, the inn guests were out on the trails in full force, and every once in a while, a little group of them would ski to the rustic lodge where Martha keeps two tremendous kettles of soup on the potbellied stove for anyone who needs to be warm. Most everyone did.

"The inn is very definitely family-style. Everyone sits around the big dining room table and there is one main dish for each meal, which Martha cooks in the farmhouse kitchen. This main dish is likely to be something quite unusual, as she is sort of a country cook with gourmet tendencies.

"The bedrooms are plain and simple with hot water bottles on the back of the doors and handsome patchwork quilts on the beds. It truly is visiting a Vermont farm in the Vermont mountains."

Well, things have really happened since 1972, and Blueberry Hill inn has become nationally famous. Tony is a recognized authority on cross-country skiing, and most avid on the subject of safety. The reservation book for winter opens on September first, and it's only fair to say that all the weekends are fully booked almost immediately. The rustic warmup lodge has been replaced by a large ski-touring center.

I'd like to share with you a letter from Martha, telling about *summer* at Blueberry Hill: "We're open from June through October

as well as from December through March for skiing. Summertime here in the Green Mountains is just fabulous. My vegetable and flower gardens are the best they've ever been. Guests gave a hand to Tony while he took down two nearby barns. Our little restaurant went off very well, with Elsie doing a super job with busy crowds on Saturday nights. Tony, by the way, does the omelets on Sunday nights.

"There's great fishing in our streams, hiking, and biking, and nearby tennis, and always a refreshing dip in the pond (I'll bet you didn't even know we had one!). Many guests who don't have their own gardens enjoy helping us pick the vegetables from ours. They can even help clear trails."

In late July, for the last two years, there has been an annual cross-country footrace and Blueberry Festival. The course covers 6.5 miles on the paved and gravel roads leading the runner down through the cool shaded heart of Goshen, Vermont, up a series of hills and back through the woods and pastures with beautiful views of the Green Mountains. Following the race the Blueberry Festival, open to competitors and spectators alike, features a chicken barbeque with salads, homemade breads, and blueberry baked goods. An old-time square dance wraps up the evening's festivities.

Besides being one of the oldest and best-known ski touring centers in Vermont, Blueberry Hill is now very popular with summer and fall back-packers and hikers. There are many, many trails, most of which are used for cross-country skiing in the wintertime. It's possible to use the inn as a central point for such activities or to include it on an itinerary. It's always important to phone ahead for reservations and information.

A few important observations about Blueberry Hill: there are no babysitting facilities for young children. Reservations for winter accommodations should be made as early as possible, as the inn is often booked solid for weeks at a time in winter.

BLUEBERRY HILL, Goshen, Vt. 05733; 802-247-6735. A mountain inn passionately devoted to cross-country skiing, 8 mi. from Brandon. Modified American plan omits lunch. All rooms with private baths. Meals not served to travelers. Open from June to November; December to April. Closed Christmas. Swimming, fishing, and xc skiing on the grounds. Tony and Martha Clark, Innkeepers.

Directions: At Brandon, travel east on Rte. 73 through Forest Dale. Then follow signs to Blueberry Hill.

OLD NEWFANE INN
Newfane, Vermont

I first heard of Eric Weindl and his wife Gundy because of the cuisine at the Old Newfane Inn. However, my visit convinced me that this historic hostelry has several other highly attractive aspects that make it an ideal objective for country inn enthusiasts.

Eric, like his fellow countryman Guenther Weinkopf at the Queen Anne Inn in Chatham, Massachusetts, originally came from a small village near Munich, and both he and Gundy speak English with a very intriguing southern German accent.

I was visiting in the middle of a warm August afternoon, just a few minutes before Eric would find it necessary to start preparations for the evening meal. The three of us were seated on the side porch overlooking the village green, the fountain, the maples and oaks, and the Windham County Courthouse.

The Courthouse was built in 1825, the same year the inn was moved to its present location from the top of Newfane hill, which at that time was really the center of the village. The Town Hall is a mixture of Greek Revival and Colonial, and there are several other buildings around the square that are much older.

I had just been escorted on a tour through every one of the ten meticulously decorated and furnished lodging rooms. It was like visiting a Vermont farmhouse of a hundred years ago. There were elaborate samplers and wall hangings such as I have never seen before. The second-floor rooms, at one time part of a ballroom, are light and airy and there's a very pleasant little side balcony overlooking the green.

Eric, who was trained as a chef in one of the best hotels in Switzerland, warmed up to the subject of the Old Newfane Inn menu, "I think we could be characterized basically as Swiss-Continental," he said. "Our maitre d' does such dishes as chateaubriand or one of several flaming specialties at the tableside, which is always a lot of fun."

"This I can tell you," said Gundy, "Eric is a very good-natured man who loves good fun, but he takes cooking very seriously and is most particular about everything on the menu, including frog legs, shrimp scampi, lobster, tournedos of beef, and medallions of veal. He is too modest to say this, but people drive for many, many miles just to enjoy dinner with us. You see, I'm the hostess so I meet them all."

Dinner was served in the low-ceilinged dining room with its mellowed beams overhead and windows along one side. The floorboards of varying widths were highly polished and there were pink tablecloths with white undercloths, candles on the table, and pistol-handled knives. The maitre d' was wearing an elegant-looking tuxedo, and the waitresses were wearing black uniforms trimmed in white.

I was entranced with the salad which was very simple and served with one of the most extraordinary, but simple, dressings I have ever tasted—just my preference for salads. I've never tasted better calves' liver which was served in a Tyrolean sauce, and I had the opportunity to sample the medallions of veal served with creamy mushrooms that were delicious. Everything could be cut with a fork.

Because both Eric and Gundy are highly involved throughout the day with food and dining room preparation, casual visitors cannot be accommodated for tours of the inn. If you have a reservation and find the front door locked, ring the bell and they will be delighted to show you to your room.

OLD NEWFANE INN, Court St., Newfane, Vermont 05345; 802-361-4427. A 10-room village inn 12 mi. west of Brattleboro, on Rte. 30. European plan. Lunch and dinner served to travelers during summer. Closed for rooms on Mondays. Open mid-Dec. to first of April; May to end of Oct. Closed Thanksgiving, Mother's Day. Near many downhill ski areas, Marlboro Music Festival. Backroading.

tennis, swimming, nearby. No facilities for children under 7. No credit cards. Eric Weindl, Innkeeper.

Directions: From New York: Follow 684 to 84 to Hartford; I-91 to Brattleboro, Exit 2. Follow Rte. 30 for 12 mi. to Newfane. From Boston: Follow Rte. 2 to Greenfield. I-91 to Brattleboro, Exit 2; follow Rte. 30 to Newfane.

CHESTER INN
Chester, Vermont

Betsy Guido was telling a wonderful true story about the town of Chester which really reflects its rather unique character.

Chester is an old Vermont village with many 19th-century homes and buildings, including a striking group of stone houses at the eastern end of town. It has one of the longest main streets of any village I have ever visited. Dominating the center of Chester is a Victorian building that reflects many architectural influences. The porch runs across the entire first floor and there is a second balcony over the center section. This is the Chester Inn which faces the block-long narrow village green.

Betsy and her husband Tom have been the innkeeper-owners of the Chester Inn for more than six years and it's been a marvelous experience for me to share with them the progress and innovations which have characterized their tenure.

Over the past few years Tom and Betsy have redecorated and refurnished every one of the attractive bedrooms, and Tom has proven himself to be an exceptional chef specializing in many veal dishes.

In 1981 they opened the Van Gogh Cafe and Lounge which is decorated with some of Vincent's prints and art books. They offer lunch and exotic snacks every day except Saturday and Sunday.

The pool area is the summertime focal point. It's such a luxurious feeling to relax around the pool reading and simply basking in the sun. The tennis courts nearby are ever waiting. If guests come without rackets and balls, the inn can supply same. Tennis has become so popular that the inn hosted the town tennis tournament this past year.

Betsy was very excited about the fact that Tater Hill in nearby Windham, a beautiful golf course located in a high, picturesque setting, has proved to be very popular with the inn guests. It becomes a good 15-kilometer cross-country ski area in the winter.

Nine miles in the other direction, a racquetball club has opened and guests may feel free to use that as well.

There are five good downhill ski areas nearby and a couple of them have snowmaking on the top in case there should be a sparse supply of snow in the wintertime.

Bicycling, too, is very popular in this section of Vermont because there are gentle foothills nearby. In fact the inn, in keeping with the fact that so many people are becoming "body conscious," has put in a sauna and exercise room, much welcomed by both cyclists and skiers of all kinds. But, I've digressed, so let's return to Betsy's story:

"In the last part of the 19th century, Chester was plagued by a series of fifty imaginative burglaries. These crimes baffled local authorities and provided gossip for over a generation. Leading the posse and offering reward money from his own pocket was Clarence Adams, the town's leading citizen. He was first selectman, chairman of the bank and a member of the state legislature.

"Would you believe that this man turned out to be the 'Chester Mystery Man'? No one in the town could believe it. There was a spectacular trial and he was found guilty. He was taken away to the state prison and from there he staged one of the great escapes of the century.

"He hypnotized himself to appear dead and with the aid of a confederate, exchanged places with a 'look-alike' cadaver from the nearby Hanover Medical School. From there he escaped to Canada and never again returned to Chester."

So we see that appearances are often deceiving. Chester, with that long street, both sides of which are graced with beautiful homes and tidy shops, would appear to have much more of a history than we can fathom at first glance. The Chester Inn has undoubtedly played a considerable role in town affairs and bids fair to be a village focal point for many years to come.

CHESTER INN, Chester, Vt. 05143; 802-875-2444. A 30-room village inn on Rte. 11, 8 mi. from Springfield, Vt. Convenient to several Vt. ski areas. Lodgings include breakfast. Dinner served to travelers daily except Mon. Lunch served in the Van Gogh Room daily except Sat. and Sun. Closed from late October to mid-November and April to mid-May. Pool, tennis, sauna and exercise room, guest privileges at nearby racquetball club, and bicycles rented on grounds. Golf, horseback riding, Alpine and xc skiing nearby. No pets. Tom and Betsy Guido, Innkeepers.

Directions: From I-91 take Exit 6. Travel west on Rte. 103 to Rte. 11.

KEDRON VALLEY INN
South Woodstock, Vermont

"I was born right across the street," said Paul Kendall. "In fact, Barbara and I are two homegrown products who have never left home." We were sitting on the porch of the Kedron Valley Inn waving at the occasional cars that make the big bend out in front. In the quiet we could hear the Kedron Brook blending with the sounds of the early evening bird calls. I got up to take a look at the box elder tree which is very rare even for that part of the country. Paul said that he was afraid that it only had a couple of more years.

We rocked our way through the twilight as the green of the mountains on both sides melted into the deep blue of the night sky.

The inn, as well as the annex, is built of beautiful dark red brick with very white mortar. Paul told me that the annex was for many years the store and post office in South Woodstock. The old safe is still built into the wall. The inn has operated continuously since 1822.

Paul and Barbara and their two active sons are living symbols of the new Vermont — young people with knowledge and spirit that see great opportunities in preserving the Vermont of yesteryear while at the same time providing modern, sensible conveniences which make it even more attractive. The KVI is tucked away in a mountain fastness near Calvin Coolidge's birthplace. However, Paul and Barbara are not content to get by on pastoral charm and Yankee reputation alone. They take pains to serve good food and continually look for ways to improve the inn.

I wrote the above paragraphs in the 1968 edition of this book, and everything is true now except that there is a great deal more going on at the Kedron Valley Inn. Besides lounging near cozy fireplaces, the winter activities include paddle tennis, ice skating, cross-country skiing, and sleigh rides on the premises, and downhill skiing at several nearby ski areas.

A few years ago the inn beeame involved in a very old Vermont tradition, that of maple sugaring. Much of this is done in the old-fashioned way using a team of horses with a sled for gathering the sap. Chip Kendall, who is now 24, is in charge of the sugaring operation.

On a recent visit, during the first snowfall of the season, the inn never looked better. The porches had been rebuilt and all the wood-trim painted, but unfortunately, the box elder tree is no more. Besides the two sleeping rooms with fireplaces, there are three more sleeping rooms with old-fashioned woodburning stoves which add additional heat and more atmosphere.

The past fifteen years have seen continuing development of opportunities for summertime diversions: one is the acre-and-a-half pond with a sandy beach and diving board, and another is the Kedron Valley Stables, with mounts for beginners and experts, private lessons, wagon rides, picnic trail rides, and horse trekking.

In line with the continuing and growing interest in horses, the KVI has for the last few years sponsored an "Inn-to-Inn" riding adventure which includes overnight stops at several farms as well as two other inns in this book. There are also weekend riding vacations with western or eastern tack, consisting of two full days of guided trail riding on dirt roads and through woodland trails. For complete information on both of those special programs please contact the inn directly.

KEDRON VALLEY INN, Rte. 106, South Woodstock, Vt. 05071; 802-457-1473. A 34-room rustic resort-inn, 5 mi. south of Woodstock. Near Killington, Mt. Ascutney ski areas. European plan. Breakfast, lunch, and dinner served daily from early May to Nov. 1.

Closed Sunday evenings Nov. to mid-March. Closed from mid-March to early May. Christmas Day buffet served from 1 to 5 p.m. Swimming, riding, sleigh rides, carriage rides, paddle tennis, hiking, and xc skiing on grounds. Tennis, golf, and bicycles nearby. Paul and Barbara Kendall, Innkeepers.

Directions: Take Exit 1 from I-89 and follow Rte. 4 to Woodstock. Proceed south on Rte. 106 for 5 mi. Or, take Exit 8 from I-91 and follow Rte. 131 for 8 mi. Proceed North on Rte. 106 for 12 mi.

I had followed Route 30 from Manchester Center through Dorset to Pawlet and then turned right on Route 133 to continue on up the valley through the wonderful remote ruralness of Vermont which never seemed more handsome than on this early winter's evening with its recently-fallen deep snow. There were surprise villages and hamlets and roads that had been plowed, but happily not salted. Kids were playing fox and geese in the snow, and perhaps most wonderful of all were the lovely weathered Vermont barns with cows patiently waiting to be milked.

THE MIDDLETOWN SPRINGS INN
Middletown Springs, Vermont

Christmastime at the Middletown Springs Inn . . . what a joy! Snow was piled at least sixteen inches deep on the tops of the hedges and the old-fashioned wheelbarrow on the lawn assumed a shape fantastical. Mel Hendrickson had carefully shoveled out a path to the handsome Victorian front door flanked by colorful Christmas decorations and I could see the lights from a Christmas tree in the main living room. As for the rest of the village, most of which has nestled around the green for decades, there were Christmas lights in every window and festoons of gay bulbs over the doors and trees. It was truly a Christmas idyll.

Before my hand had touched the graceful brass knob, the door was flung open and there were Mel and Jean Hendrickson. "Welcome to the Middletown Springs Inn and Merry Christmas!" I was immediately taken in tow and ushered into a handsome library which was warmed by an old-fashioned cast iron stove. A cup of tea and freshly made cake were placed before me, and I knew at long last I had arrived home.

The guest visiting here for the first time is surprised and then really overwhelmed by one important feature of this inn—its truly amazing collection of *dolls*.

Jean's grandmother started the collection, which was continued

by her mother and now by Jean. There are dolls everywhere—dolls of every description, shape, nationality, and occupation. It is a veritable museum of dolls. There are Dionne quintuplet dolls, Little Women dolls, Henry VIII and all of his wives—there is a doll for practically every occasion and it would be very easy to go on for paragraphs describing them, but let me tell you about Mel and Jean.

After having raised six children, they would certainly have been entitled to take life more casually. But the opportunity came to convert this Victorian mansion into an inn about three years ago and Mel and Jean viewed it as an entirely new career. They plunged in with hearts high and a youthful outlook. Now they have integrated themselves into the community. "We love it," says Jean.

There are seven very tastefully decorated Victorian bedrooms with many interesting, unusual touches, and of a certainty many dolls and other fascinating knickknacks.

A full breakfast is served which might include blueberry pancakes, sticky buns, country-style oatmeal, scrambled eggs with onions, or blueberry coffee cake. This is included in the price of the room.

The evening meal (served only to houseguests) has a single main dish such as a roast, or chicken baked with ham and cheese, and homemade desserts including "mile-high" strawberry pie.

Although I was tremendously pleased and impressed with being in Middletown Springs during the Christmas season, Mel remarked, "We are in the true sense of the word a 'holiday inn' because we decorate the inn not only for Christmas, but for Thanksgiving,

Easter, Fourth of July, Halloween, and Valentine's Day. We also might include some offbeat holidays such as St. Swithin's Day."

"Memorial Day is something special," chimed in Jean. "The town has a parade with a local marching band, floats, and decorated bikes. From our front porch we have an excellent view. It's really hometown U.S.A."

When the Hendricksons moved from Baltimore to Middletown Springs, they brought not only this fabulous collection of dolls and antiques, but also dozens and dozens of photographs of the family, including their grandparents and grandchildren, all of which are in evidence throughout the inn. It is really like being in someone's home.

This spirit is particularly true in the big kitchen where eventually everyone gathers. Attached to the refrigerator were at least five "thank you" notes painfully printed with colored crayon from their grandchildren who had joined the Hendrickson family for a reunion over Thanksgiving.

Boy, can you imagine what it's like to have Mel and Jean for grandparents and to visit them with all of the wonderful surprises in their big country home!

THE MIDDLETOWN SPRINGS INN, Middletown Springs, Vermont 05757; 802-235-2198. A 7-room Victorian mansion on the green of a lovely 18th- and 19th-century village. Shared baths. Breakfast included; arrangements can be made for dinner. Open year-round; however, call in advance for reservations. Within easy driving distance of all central Vermont summer and winter recreation in Mt. Killington, state parks, summer theater, etc. Lawn sports on grounds; swimming, golf, tennis nearby. Not suitable for young children. Jean and Mel Hendrickson, Innkeepers.

Directions: From Manchester Center, Vermont, follow Rte. 30 to Pawlet and turn north on Rte. 133 to Middletown Springs. From Poultney, Vermont follow Rte. 140 to East Poultney and on to Middletown Springs.

BIRCH HILL INN
Manchester, Vermont

Jim and Pat Lee and I were enjoying a cup of tea in the low-ceilinged living room of Birch Hill Inn. From the windows on three sides the fields, now deep under a blanket of Vermont snow, stretched down into the valley and up to the hills beyond. It was a warm, comfortable place with a spinet piano, an ongoing, never-ending jigsaw puzzle, and innumerable books and magazines. Over the big fireplace was a print of George Washington's triumphal

entry into New York City after the Revolutionary War. I noted much interest in art, music and history in this lovely old farmhouse, the main part of which is 190 years old. Four generations of Pat's family have lived here and that is one of the things that makes this inn special.

"I can see that there's lots of cross-country-skiing," I said, reaching down to pet the two golden retrievers, Abby who is seven months old and Tasha who is thirteen years of age. "Tell me about the summertime."

Jim's face lit up. "For one thing, we offer a kidney-shaped swimming pool and a view in all directions of the surrounding mountains. We have great walking trails, which are the cross-country ski trails in the winter. We have our own trout pond stocked with six- to seven-inch rainbows and the guests are allowed to catch and release the fish. It's an ideal spot to practice fly casting. Nearby, the golf is first-rate at the Equinox Golf Club and there's tennis, biking, and fabulous backroading in the mountains."

Pat picked up the conversational ball. "Our accommodations include a full breakfast. We like to serve homemade muffins, french toast, or egg-in-the-hole, and other hearty things. After breakfast we let our guests know what we will be serving for dinner that evening, and they can make a reservation if they'd like.

This perked up my interest and I asked about the menu. "Well, we always have homemade soup, tomato bisque for example, and home-baked bread. Our single entrées could be veal Marsala, butterflied leg of lamb, or chicken breasts Parmesan. Sometimes Jim cooks Cornish hens or a turkey on the outdoor grill. We have lots of fresh vegetables right from our garden, and always a flavorful salad. Our emphasis is on thoughtfully prepared food, including a delectable dessert to top off each evening meal. We all eat together and we really enjoy getting to know our guests as we sit around one big table.

Accommodations at this informal, family-style inn are in five extremely comfortable and cheerful bedrooms in the main house all of which have views toward the mountains, farm, and pond. They are well decorated with paintings and furniture from the family home. A nearby cottage on the grounds has been converted into an ideal family-style accommodation as well. Just off the main kitchen is a tidy little pantry with a refrigerator where houseguests can leave their own makings for lunch. It also has a bulletin board with notices about the dozens of things to do in the area.

Oddly enough, I have been passing the buildings of the Birch Hill Inn for at least 35 years because it is on a back-road shortcut to Dorset, Pawlet, and Poultney. I had always admired the handsome white house so beautifully landscaped and its situation on the top of the hill. I am delighted to find that the Lees have turned it into a gracious country inn.

BIRCH HILL INN, Box 346, West Road, Manchester, Vt. 05254; 802-362-2761. An extremely comfortable country home that has been converted into an inn. Five bedrooms in the main house plus a family cottage a few paces away. Located about 5 min. from downtown Manchester Center. Breakfast included in the cost of the room. Dinners offered to houseguests only by reservation, every night except Wed. Swimming pool, xc skiing, trout fishing, and walking trails on grounds. Alpine skiing at major areas nearby as well as tennis and golf facilities; great biking. Open after Christmas to mid-April, and May to late Oct. (be sure to make reservations). No pets. No credit cards. Pat and Jim Lee, Innkeepers.

Directions: From New York City: Taconic Parkway to U.S. 22. Turn east from Rte. 22 at your own choosing, and go north on Rte. 7 to Manchester. Fork left just beyond the Johnny Appleseed book shop on West Road and look for Birch Hill Inn 2 mi. on right. From Boston: take the Massachusetts Tpke. to I-91 to the Brattleboro Exit and continue to Manchester on Rte. 30.

INN AT SAWMILL FARM
West Dover, Vermont

It was one of those wonderful, magic nights when everything seemed to be falling beautifully into place. We were about 55 in number and the dining room at the Inn at Sawmill Farm was filled almost to overflowing with innkeepers from *Country Inns and Back Roads* enjoying a meeting being hosted by Ione, Brill, and Rodney Williams.

Even for the innkeepers who are frequently a blasé lot at times, the menu was a culinary adventure not only in the starter department, but in the main dishes as well. I shared a table with Ione Williams, Paul McEnroe from the Inn at Castle Hill in Newport, his wife Betty who is the innkeeper at the Inntowne Inn in Newport, and Rose Ann Hunter from the Morrill Place in Newburyport. We decided to share all the dishes, so there was much passing of clams Casino, the special game paté, and other first courses. This was followed by shrimp bisque soup that everyone declared to be superior. I ordered sweetbreads, but delighted in sampled morsels of the rack of lamb with an Indian sauce and other examples of chef Brill William's cuisine. When he came to the dining room in his immaculate white uniform, we all gave him a standing ovation.

The Inn at Sawmill Farm is well known not only among country-inn enthusiasts but also among country innkeepers themselves, and much time was spent touring the public rooms, the patio, tennis courts, the big pond and the beautiful grounds, as well as "oohing" and "ahing" over various lodging rooms, many of which are of post-and-beam construction with colorful chintzes and a generous application of barn board.

After dinner the story of Sawmill Farm was told by Rod and Ione and of how they had created the inn out of what Ione described as "a beautiful old farmhouse and barn." Their son Brill was trained by Ione in the kitchen and is now the head chef and officially one of the owners.

My acquaintance with the Williamses began in the late '60s, and since that time I have observed that in the lodging rooms added in various outbuildings of the original farm the textures of barn

111

siding, beams, ceilings, floors, and the picture windows combine to create a feeling of rural elegance. Rod and Ione are particularly qualified to create such a scene since he is an architect and she is an interior designer.

Several times during our overnight stay, I found a great many of the innkeepers gathered around the superb conversational piece in the main living room—a handsome brass telescope mounted on a tripod providing an intimate view of Mt. Snow rising majestically to the north.

As we all regretfully made our goodbyes the next day, one innkeeper said she thought it was such a lovely idea for the inn to keep its beautiful outdoor Christmas decorations so that at night the white lights on the bushes and trees created a wonderful fairyland atmosphere. Rod acknowledged her comment and said that the inn always kept these lights in place until Eastertime.

INN AT SAWMILL FARM, Box 8, West Dover, Vt. 05356; 802-464-8131. A 19-room country resort-inn on Rte. 100, 22 mi. from Bennington and Brattleboro. Within sight of Mt. Snow ski area. Modified American plan omits lunch. Breakfast and dinner served to travelers daily. Closed Nov. 7 through Dec. 7. Swimming, tennis, and trout fishing on grounds. Golf, bicycles, riding, snowshoeing, Alpine and xc skiing nearby. No children under 8. No pets. No credit cards. Rodney, Brill, and Ione Williams, Innkeepers.

Directions: From I-91, take Brattleboro Exit 2 and travel on Vt. Rte. 9 west to Vt. Rte. 100. Proceed north 5 mi. to inn. Or, take U.S.7 north to Bennington, then Rte. 9 east to Vt. Rte. 100 and proceed north 5 mi. to inn.

THE QUECHEE INN AT MARSHLAND FARM
Quechee, Vermont

Barbara Yaroschuk was telling a group of California innkeepers about the Quechee Inn at Marshland Farm (henceforth known as the Quechee Inn) in the mountains of central Vermont: "Summer is one of the nicest times in Vermont. Many people think of Vermont only for foliage and skiing, but summer is wonderful. A Vermont morning with the sun on the dew and the birds flying from our barn to nest in the trees, and the flights of water fowl from the wildlife preserve—just beautiful. Our inn was built in 1793, the farmstead of Colonel Joseph Marsh, the first lieutenant governor of Vermont, and we have one of the largest barns in the state on our property."

The occasion was a meeting of *CIBR* innkeepers at the Wine Country Inn in California's Napa Valley, and we were all seated on

the outer deck enjoying some brilliant morning sunshine as it burned off the valley mists that were obscuring the nearby high hills and vineyards.

This was quite a contrast to my visit to The Quechee Inn when the snow had been so high that I could not see the tops of the fences. That's when the term "Vermont winter" comes to mind. The inn is a cross-country skiing and learning center and there is lots of skating and downhill skiing as well as snowshoeing nearby. It's fun to spend an afternoon on the trails, and to return to a mug of mulled cider in front of the living room fireplace. While eating popcorn and cracking nuts, guests can muse over the very tempting dinner menu that features such dishes as leg of lamb, veal Marsala, roast duckling, and trout.

In summertime inn guests enjoy privileges at the Quechee Club and they can play two of the best golf courses in New England. The clubhouse has an outdoor pool and there is a beautiful little lake in the middle of the golf course, just right for the Sunfish, sailboats, and paddleboats. There are ten tennis courts.

For outdoor enthusiasts, there is much good hiking and bicycle riding and the inn is only about fifteen minutes from Woodstock, one of the most beautiful villages in New England.

Much of the interior of the inn reflects its late colonial ancestry and many of the bedrooms have been enhanced with four-poster and brass beds, and decorated with bird and flower prints. The view from the windows look out over the lawns, rolling countryside, corn fields, and the Wildlife Preserve. Two extremely handsome prints of the original owners are a focal point in the dining room.

The Quechee Inn is a dream come true for Mike and Barbara

Yaroschuk and their children, Scott, Christine, and Cathy. As in the case of most family-owned country inns, there are chores and duties for all concerned.

Ned Smith, our host at the California meeting, had visited the Quechee Inn earlier and he pointed out that it was just a few moments from one of the spectacular natural sights of New England, the Quechee Gorge. "Oh, yes," exclaimed Barbara, "it's such a beautiful sight with the river rushing between the high cliffs that form a sort of miniature Grand Canyon. It's only a ten-minute walk from our front door."

THE QUECHEE INN AT MARSHLAND FARM, Clubhouse Rd., Quechee, Vt. 05059; 802-295-3133. A 22-room country inn in central Vermont just a few minutes from Woodstock, Dartmouth College, and many other Vermont attractions. Breakfast and dinner served daily to travelers. Closed two weeks in April and November. Spectacular foliage, sugaring, hiking, fishing, canoeing, bird-watching, and cidering available. Historic sites, antique shops, covered bridges, and especially the Quechee Gorge all within short distance. Tennis, golf, swimming, squash, sauna, sailboats, xc and downhill skiing nearby. Michael and Barbara Yaroschuk, Innkeepers.

Directions: From intersection of Interstate 91 and 89, take 89 north to Exit 1 (Rte. 4, Woodstock-Rutland). West on Rte. 4 for 1.2 miles. Right on Clubhouse Road to Inn.

WHAT IS INNKEEPING REALLY LIKE?

"A memorable event in September was when a southwester broke our sailboat loose from its mooring. At 6:30 a.m. Elli and I and handyman Mike found ourselves standing knee-deep in the surf and faces full of spray while we tried to pull the boat up onto shore. I remember almost laughing and thinking: 'This is innkeeping?'"
—Maine

"The year in quick review. A snowless and therefore practically guestless winter, followed by a very slow spring. We began to wonder if the season would ever begin! And then came the summer and begin it did! People seemed to be on the road this summer and perhaps more so this fall. Foliage season travel seems to be on the increase, and once again we must attribute most of business to CIBR. Does anyone travel by anything else?

"One other major source of business for us has been local weddings: rehearsal dinners, wedding brunches, and lodging for family and friends. One wedding took place this Memorial Day in our field—a true country wedding complete with wildflower bouquets."
—Maine

"I imagine you must wonder how we're holding up as innkeepers after another year . . . Well, we have both changed quite a bit this year . . . I find myself to be content with my life as an innkeeper despite the fact that, at times, the last thing I want to do is answer the phone or attend to a guest. I find that I have developed a great deal of pride in the inn and what I have done here . . . I like it when people come here and enjoy the place (and to a certain extent, I have become more tolerant with those who do not) . . . I like to have people envy me, yet it worries me that I may some day become arrogant about my minor accomplishments. I often wish that I could get into the habit of setting aside a small piece of every day to just stop and be grateful for what I have. (Without being religious in the traditional sense.)— New Hampshire Continued on page 191

I do not include lodging rates in the descriptions, for the very nature of an inn means that there are lodgings of various sizes, with and without baths, in and out of season, and with plain and fancy decoration. Travelers should call ahead and inquire about the availability and rates of the many different types of rooms.

"European Plan" means that rates for rooms and meals are separate. *"American Plan"* means that meals are included in the cost of the room. *"Modified American Plan"* means that breakfast and dinner are included in the cost of the room. The rates at some inns include a continental breakfast with the lodging.

Southern New England

Eastern Time Zone

ALBANY

Millhof Inn, *Stephentown, N.Y.*

PITTSFIELD

Peirson Place, *Richmond*

Village Inn, *Lenox*

Inn at Huntington, *Huntington*

Red Lion Inn, *Stockbridge*

Colonel Ebenezer Crafts Inn, *Sturbridge*

MASSACHUSETTS

M A S S

Stagecoach Hill Inn, *Sheffield*

White Hart Inn, *Salisbury*

Mountain View Inn, *Norfolk*

HARTFORD

Boulders Inn, *New Preston*

Curtis House, *Woodbury*

Town Farms Inn, *Middletown*

C O N N E C T I C U T

West Lane Inn, *Ridgefield*

Griswold, *Essex*

NEW HAVEN

Silvermine Tavern, *Norwalk*

Homestead Inn, *Greenwich*

NEW YORK CITY

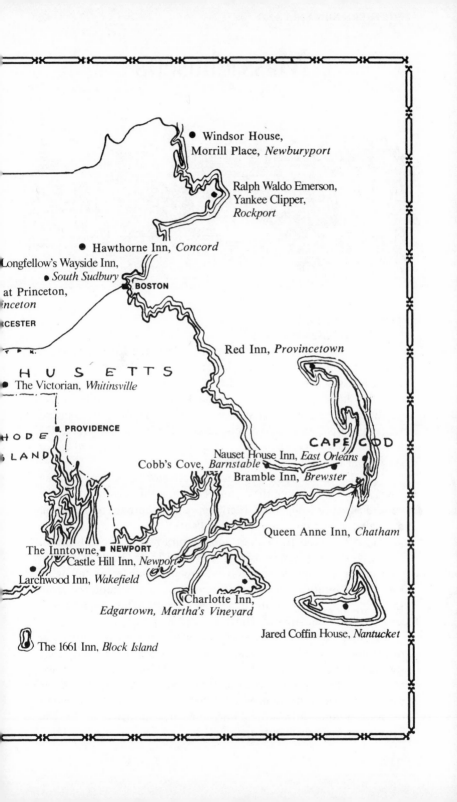

Windsor House,
Morrill Place, *Newburyport*

Ralph Waldo Emerson,
Yankee Clipper,
Rockport

Hawthorne Inn, *Concord*

Longfellow's Wayside Inn,
South Sudbury

BOSTON

at Princeton,
inceton

inceton

RCESTER

T P K.

H U S E T T S

The Victorian, *Whitinsville*

HODE

LAND

PROVIDENCE

Red Inn, *Provincetown*

CAPE COD

Nauset House Inn, *East Orleans*

Cobb's Cove, *Barnstable*

Bramble Inn, *Brewster*

Queen Anne Inn, *Chatham*

The Inntowne, NEWPORT

Castle Hill Inn, *Newport*

Larchwood Inn, *Wakefield*

Charlotte Inn,
Edgartown, Martha's Vineyard

Jared Coffin House, *Nantucket*

The 1661 Inn, *Block Island*

Massachusetts

THE RED LION INN
Stockbridge, Massachusetts

Betsy Holtzinger, the innkeeper at The Red Lion Inn, and I were seated in the Widow Bingham's Tavern, a pleasant pub room at the inn, discussing the new menu.

"We have a special New England section which will feature traditional regional dishes such as scallop and oyster pie, sautéed venison chops, and Yankee pot roast," she said. "Of course the longtime favorites such as steaks, prime ribs, veal Oscar, and baked stuffed shrimp will still be offered."

Jim Lucie, the food and beverage director, sat down, handing me my very own copy of the menu. "Of course this is going to change periodically," he said, "but it represents a new approach to the menu, particularly emphasizing American dishes."

The Red Lion Inn comes quite naturally to this emphasis on things American. It was originally erected in 1773 and used as a convention site by delegates from the many different towns of Berkshire County to protest the use of any articles imported from England. For many years it served as a stop for stagecoaches traveling between Albany, Hartford, and Boston.

In 1862, following a succession of owners, the inn was purchased by members of the Treadway family and remained in their possession for well over ninety years. Unfortunately, the building was almost completely destroyed by fire in 1896; however, it was rebuilt and has remained virtually unchanged since that time. Most of the collection of fine antique furniture, china, and pewter acquired by the Treadways is on display today.

We who live in Stockbridge were dismayed to learn in 1967 that the inn might possibly be torn down and replaced by a gasoline station. So we were much relieved when Jack and Jane Fitzpatrick, owners of Country Curtains, acquired the property. They reopened the inn in May, 1969, and it's been thriving ever since.

"We know that for many people The Red Lion is their first 'country inn experience,'" explained Betsy, "and for that reason we take a special care in seeing to it that everything is as authentically 'country inn' as possible. Mrs. Fitzpatrick is very particular about details and I believe the inn certainly shows the results of the love and interest that both she and the Senator have taken in it during these years. (Jack Fitzpatrick was at one time our state senator.)

Stockbridge is a five-season town: winter, spring, summer, autumn, and "fall foliage." In summer the area enjoys the Berkshire Music Festival at Tanglewood, as well as the Berkshire Theater Festival and Jacob's Pillow Dance Festival, all world-renowned attractions. In winter the snow-covered hills of the Berkshires make downhill and cross-country skiing a major sport. The Red Lion is but minutes from several ski-lift areas. The quiet unfolding of a Berkshire spring is something not to be missed. This is when woodland walks or the Pleasant Valley Bird Sanctuary beckon, as well as the cycling trails, or just walking on the main street of Stockbridge.

Fortunately the Norman Rockwell Museum, which contains many of his original paintings, is open year-round, every day except Tuesdays.

If I sound somewhat proprietary about The Red Lion it is because I can look from my office window up the street and see the corner of the broad porch where guests enjoy the rocking chairs in all seasons of the year.

RED LION INN, Stockbridge, Mass. 01262; 413-298-5545. A 95-room historic village inn dating back to 1773 in the Berkshire Mountains. Adjacent to Tanglewood, Norman Rockwell's Old Corner House Museum. The Berkshire Playhouse, Jacob's Pillow, Chesterwood Gallery, Mission House, and major ski areas. European plan. Breakfast, lunch, and dinner. Open year-round. (From Nov. 1 to May 1, only 30 rooms open.) Outdoor heated pool. Tennis, golf, boating, fishing, hiking, mountain climbing, and xc skiing nearby. Jack and Jane Fitzpatrick, Owners; Betsy Holtzinger, Innkeeper.

Directions: From the Taconic State Pkwy, take Exit 23 (N.Y. Rte. 23) to Mass. Rte. 7. Proceed north to Stockbridge. From the Mass. Tpke. Exit #2 Lee, follow Rte. 102 to Stockbridge.

LONGFELLOW'S WAYSIDE INN
South Sudbury, Massachusetts

I'll never, NEVER forget that night. There must have been at least forty innkeepers from *CIBR* enjoying a roast goose dinner in the upstairs dining room of Longfellow's Wayside Inn. We were having the fun of getting together and the opportunity to recognize innkeeper Frank Koppeis as the New England Innkeeper of the year.

We had gathered at lunch earlier that afternoon, and had spent a very pleasant few hours talking over innkeeping problems and exchanging ideas, and then had gone on a tour of the special sights at the Wayside, including the Old Gristmill, the Martha and Mary Chapel where so many people were married every year, the Little Red Schoolhouse, and the many very special, well-preserved bedrooms of this hostelry which actually dates back well into the 18th century.

Between the soup and salad I became aware of a sound in the hallway beyond the dining room and then, without warning, the door burst open and there immediately paraded into the room about seventeen men and boys wearing Colonial costumes and playing fifes and drums! The sound of their music and the jauntiness of their spirit filled the dining room and everyone arose and applauded vigorously. Of course, we had all been filled with the fascinating history of Sudbury and the fact that the militiamen had marched off to nearby Concord on April 18, 1775, to participate in the events that are so well-known to every student of American history.

Now with this great stirring music being played by piccolos, fifes, and drums and with the musicians, even the young boys, all dressed in Colonial costume, there was no doubt that we felt as if "we were there."

120

This is the Sudbury Ancient Fife and Drum Company and they stayed on long enough to play about four numbers and joked with us considerably and told us a little bit about what they do and the fact that they have been playing in this band for a long time and make appearances all over the country. They marched off to the tune of "The Girl I left Behind Me," which has been a popular tune since long before the American Revolution. I'm happy to report that the Fife and Drum Company play on the road in front of the inn Wednesday evenings during the summer, which also serves as a practice session for them.

What else can I say now about Longfellow's Wayside Inn? Incidentally, this building which has had many trials and tribulations of its own, is now in the hands of a foundation that is interested in preserving it in perpetuity. It was discovered by Henry Longfellow during the 19th century and I'm sure that all of us are familiar with the almost-epic poem that deals with some of the habitués of that time. In the early twenties Henry Ford also heavily endowed it.

There are a few lodging rooms available, but please, to avoid disappointment, make reservations well in advance. The dining room specializes in good New England fare such as baked Cape Cod scallops, Indian pudding served with ice cream, muffins made from meal stone ground at the Gristmill, and Massachusetts duckling in orange sauce.

It's a great experience even when the Fife and Drum Corps is *not* making an appearance!

LONGFELLOW'S WAYSIDE INN, Wayside Inn Rd., off Rte. 20, South Sudbury, Mass. 01776; 617-443-8846. A 10-room historic landmark inn, midway between Boston and Worcester. Within a short distance of Concord, Lexington, and other famous Revolutionary War landmarks. European plan. Lunch and dinner served daily except Christmas. Breakfast served to overnight guests. Francis Koppeis, Innkeeper.

Directions: From the west, take Exit 11A from Mass. Tpke. and proceed north on 495 to Rte. 20. Follow Rte. 20 7 mi. east to inn. From the east, take Exit 49 from Rte. 128. Follow Rte. 20 west 11 mi. to inn.

THE HAWTHORNE INN
Concord, Massachusetts

In previous editions of this book, I've suggested that Gregory Burch is a real Renaissance man, equally at home at the easel, with sculptors' clay, at an archeological dig, or entertaining his guests at the morning breakfast table. I've also suggested that at The

Hawthorne Inn he is carrying on the literary and artistic thrust of 19th-century Concord.

All of that is true, except for one important change. Gregory Burch and Marilyn Mudry were married on the evening of August 5th, 1981, and the Hawthorne Inn can now boast a Renaissance woman as well!

A few words are in order about The Hawthorne Inn. It is located down the road from the Alcott House on the road out of Concord toward Lexington. Gregory and Marilyn will be happy to explain its connections with Nathaniel Hawthorne. It is tucked back a short ways from the road with many beautiful 100-year-old maples and larches which were planted by Hawthorne.

Now let me share a few words in a letter I had from Marilyn. "Our wedding was beautiful. We moved all of our indoor plants outside to the pond area and constructed a small place for Gregory and me to stand." (She enclosed a photograph showing the two of them looking positively blissful!) "There were just a few people at the wedding, but later on we had a large party. Sorry you couldn't be there.

"We've been clearing out the wooded area in the back of the house and landscaping it. Our bees are doing just fine and our dogs love being inn-dogs. They are constantly going for walks with the guests. I'm almost finished with new quilts for all of the beds. I am now doing all of the baking and I'm thinking about doing a small bread cookbook with drawings by Gregory. I always seem to be writing out recipes, so why not a book?

"We now have six guest rooms and four baths. All of the doors have name-plaques on them and scented wreaths. There are dried flowers in the rooms, am-fm clock radios, fresh fruit, poetry books, and herbal sachets. We offer people tea or coffee as they check in. About 90% of our furnishings are now antiques. We have many oriental rugs; they go very well with the Japanese prints and Gregory's prints and carvings.

"When your book comes out, Gregory and I will have returned from a long stay in Peru and perhaps other South American countries. We have a friend coming to take care of the dogs, cats, and the house.

"Our recent research indicates that the land was once owned by Emerson, Alcott, and Hawthorne, and we have some larch trees planted on the west side by Hawthorne. We also think Alcott had his boathouse in the backyard and are trying to find the exact spot so we can build a reproduction.

"We just love being innkeepers and this is our home and we try to instill an atmosphere of peace, heavenly thought, relaxation, and a caring for our fellow man."

I feel that anything I might add to Marilyn's letter would be redundant, and I'm sure that Hawthorne, Alcott, and Emerson would all agree.

THE HAWTHORNE INN, 462 Lexington Road, Concord, Mass. 01742; 617-369-5610. A 6-room bed-and-breakfast village inn approximately 19 mi. from Boston. Breakfast to houseguests is the only meal served. Closed in January and February. Within walking distance of all of the historic and literary points of interest in Concord. No pets. No credit cards. Limited facilities for young children, but ideal for young people who have an appreciation for history and literature. Gregory Burch, Marilyn Mudry, Innkeepers.

Directions: The Hawthorne Inn is in the historic zone of Concord, ¾ of a mi. east of the town center. From Rte. 128-95 take Exit 45 west for 3 mi. Bear right at the single blinking yellow light. The inn is one mi. farther on the left (south side), directly across from the Wayside (home of Hawthorne and Alcott).

ROCKPORT, MASSACHUSETTS

Rockport has been an artists' colony for over forty years. Once it was a sleepy fishing village, but then it was "discovered" by artists during the Depression of the thirties. Some of the most important people in painting have either visited or lived in Rockport. Now it attracts all kinds of creative people, including photographers, writers, and craftsmen, as well as artists.

The Rockport Art Association's annual exhibitions are always a big event. Rockport has been referred to as one of America's most paintable locations with its open ocean, snug harbors, picturesque fishing boats, and great, gorgeous rocks.

The town is filled with fetching little houses with beguiling roof lines, inviting gardens, and winding, elm-shaded streets. Furthermore, I am sure there must be at least a hundred different fascinating shops in this little seaside community.

How fortunate it is that the railroad from Boston has several trains each day.

YANKEE CLIPPER
Rockport, Massachusetts

The granite boulders loomed around me as I gingerly negotiated the rocky path, grateful that I had worn my rubber-soled deck shoes. With the aid of some strategically placed rope railings, and following Fred Wemyss's directions, I picked my way down to the water's edge. On this warm September morning it was like a totally different world. There were small tidal pools in which I could see bright green moss and several species of marine life. Overhead a few gulls dipped and swooped, bright spots of white against the clear blue sky. I sat with my back against a warm granite boulder, enjoying the sun and salty sea air.

At dinner the previous evening I had heard the whole story of the inn. In 1946, Fred and Lydia Wemyss were here on vacation, when the idea of turning a private estate into an inn occurred to them. They have been here ever since.

"These have been wonderful years for us," Fred told me. "Our son, Gary, and our daughter, Barbara Ellis, now our assistant innkeeper, have both grown up here. Gary stayed in the innkeeping business with us and is the manager of the Ralph Waldo Emerson in Pigeon Cove. The most satisfactory part of innkeeping has been the hundreds of people who have become good friends." Because

124

Fred and Lydia are so warm and outgoing, many of the guests have been returning year after year.

I was very pleased to learn Debbie Tallett from the Millhof Inn (*CIBR*) spent the summer at the Yankee Clipper on a work-study program given for credit by the Berkshire Community College where she is studying Hotel Management. She did a great job in the kitchen assisting the cooks and her homemade breads and carrot cake made a big hit. Barbara Ellis hopes that Debbie will be with them in 1982 as well.

The inn complex consists of three buildings. The first is the original building overlooking the water where the dining area is located, and where there are many large rooms with a sea view. A few paces away, there is the Quarter Deck where some of the rooms enjoy an unobstructed view of the ocean and gardens. The third is called the Bullfinch House and is noted particularly for its architectural beauty. It is of colonial Greek·design, named for its designer who also created the Boston State House.

My reverie was broken by a sailboat's passing not fifty yards from where I sat sunning myself. I decided to return to the inn and went back up the path to the grassy lawn with its carefully tended flower beds, the beautiful terrace, and the grape arbor. Lunch was being served under the shade of the old New England apple trees.

Speaking of food, the Sunday night buffet at the Yankee Clipper consists of seafood Newburg on patty shells, or chicken a la king, or perhaps beef Stroganoff; tossed salad, green peas, tomato aspic, or molded fruit salad, and various condiments. Dessert is fruit cup or prunes plus cinammon pinapple chunks with homemade cakes.

In some ways Fred Wemyss sums up the hospitality at the Yankee Clipper with one of his typical limericks:

> "A seasoned old traveler named Flynn
> Said, 'of all of the places I've been
> To wine in, to dine in,
> To have a good time in,
> You can't beat an old country inn.'"

YANKEE CLIPPER, Rockport, Mass. 01966; 617-546-3407. An intimate 28-room inn on the sea, 40 mi. from Boston. European plan available year-round. Modified American plan from May 15 to July 1 and Labor Day to Nov. 1. Bed and continental breakfast rates available upon request. The Quarter Deck is open Thurs. through Sun., Nov. 1 to April 1. Breakfast and dinner served daily. Lunch served during July and August. Meals served to travelers by reservation only. Ocean view, shoreline walks, many antique shops and other stores nearby. No pets. Fred and Lydia Wemyss, Innkeepers.

Directions: Take I-95 to Rte. 128 to 127 (Gloucester). Proceed 6 mi. on Rte. 127 to Rockport and continue to Pigeon Cove.

RALPH WALDO EMERSON
Rockport, Massachusetts

The telephone call came from Ohio and the man on the other end had this to say: "I've lived out here in the Midwest all of my life, and one of the things I've always wanted to do was to travel to New England and spend some time by the ocean. Where would I go to find lots of ocean and rocks to climb, where it's real 'New England'?"

I thought instantly of the Ralph Waldo Emerson. Its broad veranda has an unobstructed view of the ocean and it has some of the best climbing rocks that can be found anywhere.

The "Emerson," as it's called in Pigeon Cove, is made for people who are fascinated by the sea. It is possible to walk from that broad front porch across the lawn, through the natural rock garden, across a little dirt road to the rocks on the shore. And what rocks they are! A marvelous collection of boulders and great slabs of granite which are relics of the ice age. Among them are hundreds of small tidal pools. The sea gulls dive and zoom continually. Offshore there are dozens of little buoys which indicate where the lobster traps are in the waters below.

I tried to explain all of this as lucidly as possible. He asked me if they served typical New England food. "Well," I replied, "How do lobster, clams, fresh saltwater fish, and homemade cakes sound to you?" He agreed.

I told him about Pigeon Cove and strolling along the tree-shaded streets with the rambler roses and the New England houses. I explained about the lanes that led down to the sea to provide access to the rockbound coast, and how much they reminded me of lanes in Sussex and Surrey, which for centuries have provided a path between the fields and into the woods.

To his inquiry about whether children would like it, I replied that when I was there last, a fair number were in evidence. "They enjoy the pool at the ocean," I pointed out.

I explained that the Emerson was really the result of putting two resort hotels together and making them into one. It is more like a hotel than an inn as far as the atmosphere is concerned, but because it is owned by the Wemyss family who also operates the Yankee Clipper, there is very much of the feeling of personal hospitality. I most enjoy sitting on the broad veranda which overlooks the ocean during the clement months, and the comfortable living room during the rest of the year. There are lots of opportunities to get acquainted with other guests, and Gary Wemyss is very much the genial innkeeper.

Before he rang off, he asked whether Ralph Waldo Emerson, the famous New England essayist, had ever stayed at the inn. "They say he did," I answered. "In his diary he made this entry: 'Returned from Pigeon Cove where we made the acquaintance of the sea for seven days. 'Tis a noble, friendly power and seemed to say to me: "Why so late and slow to come to me? Am I not here always thy proper summer home"?'"

"Well," he replied, "if it is good enough for Ralph Waldo Emerson, I think it certainly will be good enough for me. I am going to make my reservations for July right now."

RALPH WALDO EMERSON, 1 Cathedral Ave., Rockport, Mass. 01966; 617-546-6321. A 36-room oceanside inn, 40 mi. from Boston. Modified American and European plans. Breakfast and dinner served daily from July 1 to Labor Day; bed and breakfast only during remainder of the year. Pool, sauna, and whirlpool bath on grounds. Tennis, golf nearby. Courtesy car. No pets. Gary Wemyss, Innkeeper.

Directions: Take I-95 to Rte. 128 to 127 (Gloucester). Proceed 6 mi. on Rte. 127 to Rockport and continue to Pigeon Cove.

THE VICTORIAN
Whitinsville, Massachusetts

I was having lunch at the Victorian on the sun porch, which has been beautifully decorated and furnished in a kind of Sadie Thompson-cum-Art Nouveau motif. We sat in the fabulous white wicker South Sea Island chairs amidst a collection of hanging plants which Martha Flint identified as Swedish ivy, Wandering Jew, and

Boston fern. "Everybody wants to sit out here," she said. "It's so wonderfully bright, especially with windows on three sides."

The cover of the luncheon menu, like the dinner and dessert menus, was adapted from designs of the 1920s showing very modish men and women looking as if they had all stepped out of a page of a French fashion magazine of the time.

It was the *inside,* however, that interested me most, and the choice today included several types of omelets, including crabmeat and cream cheese, spinach and sour cream; a variety of salads, crêpes, coquilles St. Jacques, and eggs Victorian.

While I was at it, I also took a peek at the dinner menu featuring "Medallions of the Huntress," which the menu described as two small filets of beef with a classic brown sauce. There were also prime ribs of beef, scallops gratinée, duckling served with sweet and sour sauce and garnished with a peach mousse, veal Oscar, filet of sole, and shrimp scampi.

"Our first course, which is included with each dinner, is described by the waiter or waitress. We prefer to serve salads after dinner in the continental manner," Orin explained.

The dessert menu included crêpes, cheesecake, apricot sherbet, brandy Alexander pie, chocolate mousse, and lime Bavarian pie. An additional menu described the various kinds of coffees and after-dinner specialties, such as Irish coffee, café Amaretto di amore, café chocolat anisette, and café Caribbean; all of these had short descriptions to help the relatively uninitiated, such as myself.

The Victorian is an imposing mansion that sits regally above the road on a grassy slope. There is rich wood paneling everywhere and appropriate, somewhat massive Victorian furniture. Unusual touches include hand-tooled leather wainscoting in a charming third-floor room with lovely arched windows, and intricately tiled floors in the bathrooms.

Some of the eight bedrooms have walk-in closets, and one has a dressing room with full-length mirrors mounted on the mahogany doors. Little "extras" at the Victorian include apples in the guests' rooms, turn-down service, hot mulled wine, and a continental breakfast for houseguests. The recently-painted exterior has been graced with real awnings and flower beds.

I'm certain that the Whitin family, who built this beautiful mansion during the 19th century and for whom the town is named, would thoroughly approve of the warm spirit of hospitality that pervades it today.

THE VICTORIAN, 583 Linwood Ave., Whitinsville, Mass. 01588; 617-234-2500. An 8-room (6 with private baths) Victorian mansion in a quiet town 15 mi. from Worcester, Ma. and 40 mi. from Narragansett Bay in R.I. European plan. Dinner served to travelers daily except Mondays. Lunch served to travelers Tues. thru Fri. Open on Sun. at 5 p.m. Overnight guests receive continental breakfast. Lawn games, ice skating, fishing on grounds. Golf and tennis nearby. Pets accepted. Orin and Martha Flint, Innkeepers.

Directions: From Providence, follow Rte. 146 north and take the Uxbridge exit. From the traffic light in Uxbridge, proceed north on Rte. 122 approximately 1½ mi. to Linwood Ave. (there will be a sign on the corner saying "Whitinsville—Left"). Bear left here. The inn is a few hundred yards around the corner. From Worcester, follow Rte. 146 south to the Whitinsville-Purgatory Chasm exit. Proceed into Whitinsville and keep right at the set of traffic lights onto Linwood Ave. The inn is on the left at the other end of Linwood Ave.—about 1½ mi.

STAGECOACH HILL
Sheffield, Massachusetts

I like to arrive at Stagecoach Hill just at dusk as the carefully tended stone walls along Route 41 become vague shapes, and occasionally my headlights reveal some deer out in the meadow. This route is aptly named Undermountain Road, for along this stretch I feel as if I am driving directly underneath the imposing, protective influence of Mount Race.

Entry is through ponderous Victorian doors and up a short flight of stairs to a lounge area, dimly-lit by candles flickering in red jars. Except in the warm summer months, additional light is provided by fires on two raised hearths.

More candles grace the dining rooms, which are most inviting

with their red tablecloths, white napkins and gleaming silverware. The walls have sporting and hunting prints and a generous sprinkling of photographs and prints of the English royal family, including Queen Victoria, Queen Mary, King George, and Prince Charles and Lady Diana.

The innkeepers are John and Ann Pedretti who have lived in the Berkshires for a number of years. Oddly enough, they moved to England for two years in the early 1970s, and since Ann is from Lancashire, England, they're both very pleased to have found such an English inn in such a beautiful setting. In some ways, it reminds me of a traditional English inn in Ann's own Lancashire country called, "Hark to Bounty."

In addition to doing all of the cooking, Ann also does the extremely neat lettering on the blackboard menu which on my last visit showed such interesting main courses as baked scallops, duckling Bigarade, steak and kidney pie, and roast prime rib of beef served with Yorkshire pudding. "I learned to cook several different veal dishes because John is from northern Italy and he loves them. I also do a New England oyster pie," she said. (The recipe for this pie is in our *CIBR Cookbook*.)

In looking at the menu, I realized that it offered a choice of either an à la carte or table d'hôte, or a mixture of each. Certain appetizers are offered at no additional charge, as well as certain desserts.

The "Coach," as it's known locally, is an ideal distance from either Boston or New York. Its situation in the Berkshires makes it ideal for a visit in any season, because there are several ski areas within a very short drive, and also good cross-country skiing. In summer, all of the Berkshire recreational and cultural advantages are most accessible.

During 1981 in addition to rather rustic overnight accommodations in the old red barn and a small outbuilding on the property, three new country inn bedrooms were added in the main house. These are all furnished with gay curtains and matching bedspreads and appropriate furniture. One of these rooms has its own kitchen.

Breakfast is not offered to guests at Stagecoach Hill; however, there is always a pot of coffee available.

STAGECOACH HILL INN, Undermountain Rd., Sheffield, Mass. 01257; 413-229-8585. An American country inn with British overtones located on Rte. 41 midway between Salisbury, Conn., and Gt. Barrington, Mass. Three lodging rooms in main building. Dinner served every day. Luncheons served every day from May 1 to Oct. 31. Closed Christmas Day. Near So. Berkshire ski areas, Tanglewood, Jacob's Pillow, and all summertime and winter attractions. John and Ann Pedretti, Innkeepers.

Directions: From Mass. Tpke., take Exit 2 and follow Rte. 102 west to Stockbridge. Take Rte. 7 south to Great Barrington, then follow Rte. 41 south to inn.

COLONEL EBENEZER CRAFTS INN
Sturbridge, Massachusetts

For some years I have been hoping to find an inn in central Massachusetts which could be an ideal overnight stop for travelers from the west to Boston or Maine, or from New York City and the south to New England. Oddly enough, I found it almost under my nose in Sturbridge, Massachusetts, containing one of the Bay State's most enduring and worthwhile attractions: Old Sturbridge Village, a community of early 19th-century New England which has been reproduced with taste and style.

The ten room bed-and-breakfast Ebenezer Crafts Inn (guests are invited to have luncheon and dinner at the nearby Publick House), was originally built by David Fiske in 1786. Placed by Mr. Fiske on a high point of land, the house still overlooks the rolling hills adjacent to Sturbridge. It was named for one of the early patriots of Massachusetts, Colonel Ebenezer Crafts, who later migrated to Vermont's northern kingdom where the town of Craftsbury Common commemorates his contributions to the community.

The congenial host and hostess at the Ebenezer Crafts Inn are Patricia and Henri Bibeau, who were most accommodating during my stay, and provide inn guests with a continental breakfast and an afternoon tea which is served either on the terrace overlooking the new swimming pool or in the warm living room or sunporch.

Each of the lodging rooms has its own bath and shower, and at the time of my visit, there was a bowl of apples in each room for everyone to enjoy. Pat commented that she frequently turns down the beds in the evening and also leaves cookies. Both are nice country inn touches.

The rooms are very light and airy and are furnished either in antiques or good reproductions. There were a number of chenille bedspreads, including one called "The Pride of Sturbridge."

The living room really invites guests to get acquainted and I was delighted to find a generously supplied bookcase and also stacks of the *National Geographic* which makes wonderful bedtime reading.

The nearby Publick House (the inn is actually under the same management) has a continual program of four-season activities, including Yankee Winter Weekends, celebrations on Easter, Patriots' Day, Mother's Day, Memorial Day, and other holidays. The Christmas celebration, incidentally, goes on for twelve days. Guests of the inn are invited to participate in all of these events.

I must admit that I was taken by the quiet, hideaway feeling at this inn. The Indian-red stain of the narrow clapboards which are accented by the white trim, proved an ideal setting for the elm, maple, oak, and apple trees and the many beds of flowers.

Because guests at the Colonel Ebenezer Crafts Inn take a great many of their meals at the nearby Publick House, it is of interest to know that luncheons and dinners there include excellent New England clam chowder, as well as New England dishes such as lobster pie, broiled native scallops, double-thick lamb chops, deep dish apple pie—à la mode or with cheddar cheese—and Indian pudding served with vanilla ice cream.

CIBR readers with reservations at the Ebenezer Crafts Inn should check in at the main desk of the Publick House which is in the village of Sturbridge.

COLONEL EBENEZER CRAFTS INN, c/o Publick House, Box 187, Sturbridge, Ma. 01566; 617-347-3313. A 10-room bed and breakfast inn in a historic village 18 mi. from Worcester. Old Sturbridge Village nearby. Lodging rates include continental breakfast and afternoon tea. (Lunch and dinner available at nearby Publick House.) Open year-round. Swimming pool on grounds. Tennis nearby. Buddy Adler, Innkeeper.

Directions: From Massachusetts Tpke.: take Exit 9, follow signs to Sturbridge on Rte. 131. From Hartford: follow I-84, which becomes I-86. Take Exit 3.

PEIRSON PLACE
Richmond, Massachusetts

Margaret Kingman and I were seated by the pond at the Peirson Place, and so placid was the surface that it mirrored a willow tree by the waterfall. It was early fall, and already the sugar maples, oaks, ash, hickory, birch, and walnut trees on the grounds of this delightful, historic hideaway were beginning to feel the faint touch of autumn's brush.

"I've spent years researching the history of this property," she said. "It's a Historical Landmark in Berkshire County. We have two houses here, plus a great many outbuildings—this beautiful big barn behind us, and 150 acres of wooded hillside."

Margaret warmed to the subject, "The smaller of the houses is called Cogswell and was built in 1762 by Joseph Cogswell. He had to buy it twice, once from the Indians and once from the Colonial Government Proprietors of Berkshire County. A few years later Nathan Peirson built a tannery on this land, thereby starting a connection through a later marriage between the two families. Joseph Cogswell and his four sons were minute-men serving at Bennington, Bunker Hill, and Valley Forge. Nathan Peirson was a lieutenant in the Revolutionary Army for which he supplied boots and saddle leather, and which enabled him to build a new tannery here in 1784.

"The main house was built in 1788 on the site of the first tannery, and the Cogswells and the Peirsons were united when Nathan's oldest daughter married a grandson of Joseph Cogswell.

"Many of our guests are interested in the fact that my great-grandfather, my mother, and I were all born in the same room in the Peirson House and that my family has owned the property since the land was acquired from the Indians in 1762.

"I think that the Peirson Place has probably changed very little outwardly from the steel engraving in the *History of Berkshire County,* published in 1875. Our front hall still has the original French wallpaper of 1789. Ells have been added to both houses and we have modern bathrooms, instead of 'curtained washrooms.'"

The Peirson Place is really very unusual. Within this circumference of history and natural beauty, Margaret has created an intimate bed-and-breakfast inn that is markedly different from other accommodations in the Berkshires. She has many guests who have been returning year after year because they enjoy the shaded quiet of the Victorian gazebo and the tranquility of the woods. Many follow the birdwatcher's path or the unusual trail for the blind, perhaps the only one I've ever heard of which allows sightless people to enjoy the woods and fields by "smell and tell." During my short visit, I saw many guests riding bicycles, and some were swimming in the pond and enjoying the use of the sauna.

Breakfasts or afternoon teas are great fun here because guests have been to Tanglewood, Jacob's Pillow, or the Berkshire Playhouse, or perhaps visited Williamstown, or the nearby Hancock Shaker Village, so the conversation is quite lively. The fresh croissants and crumpets disappear just about as quickly as the attractive young girls in their red-checked cobbler's aprons can bring them in.

Accommodations are in a wide variety of environments, including the main house which has very sumptuous rooms. There

are more frugal but most interesting quarters —hosteling facilities —
in the barn. "We make refrigerator space available for guests who
wish to picnic by the pond, and there are dozens of good restaurants
here in the Berkshires."

*PEIRSON PLACE, Richmond, Mass. 01254; 413-698-2750. A
10-room country house, 6 miles from Pittsfield on Rte. 41 near all of
the scenic attractions of the Berkshire hills: Tanglewood, Hancock
Shaker Village, marvelous backroading in western Massachusetts,
eastern New York, and southern Vermont. Various accommodations: 4 rooms with private baths, 6 rooms share 3 baths. Hosteling
facilities available in the barn. Lodgings include morning coffee and
pastry, afternoon tea, and all of the facilities in the woods and the
nearby fields. Open every day from Memorial Day through Labor
Day; weekends only in May and after Labor Day to Veterans' Day.
One-day rentals not accepted on weekends during Tanglewood
season. Pond, sauna, badminton, darts, boating, hiking on grounds.
Tennis, golf, horseback riding, etc., nearby. No pets. No facilities to
amuse children under 12. Margaret Mace Kingman, Innkeeper.*

*Directions: From Boston: Take Massachusetts Turnpike to Exit 1.
Follow Rte. 41 north through Richmond. Peirson Place on left-hand
side. From New York: Leave Taconic State Parkway on Rte. 295 and
continue east to Rte. 41. Turn left.*

THE QUEEN ANNE INN
Chatham, Cape Cod, Massachusetts

It's just possible that I was talking to one of the most
enthusiastic, if not one of the youngest, innkeepers of my acquaintance.
She was wearing yellow jogging pants, a blue striped top, and blue
jogging shoes. Her name was Sonja Weinkopf and she was all of
thirteen years old. Her father and mother, Guenther and Nicole, are
the innkeepers of the Queen Anne Inn which can be found in
Chatham on Cape Cod.

Sonja and I were having an early morning conversation on a
deck in the rear of the inn which overlooks a spacious lawn where
some chairs and benches have been placed under the trees, making it
a very inviting prospect for reading and enjoying quiet moments.
Attractive guest cottages are nestled among the trees.

The original center portion of this grey-shingled, blue-shuttered
inn was built in 1840 by sea captain Solomon Howes as a wedding
present for his daughter, and was later to become a parsonage.
Named the Queen Anne Inn in 1930, it began an interesting new life
as a restaurant and lodging place, serving the public since its
opening day.

In the winter of 1978 Guenther, in association with Siegfried Kiesewetter, restored and renovated the building and these two men, both from Austria, are bringing what appears to be the best of European innkeeping tradition into a perfect marriage with some of the delightful ambience of the outer Cape. Siegfried is in charge of the dining and service, and among the continental touches is the custom of placing only silverware for each individual course on the table at one time.

The staff is very friendly, and is composed largely of young women from the same sorority at Dickinson College in Carlisle, Pennsylvania. Ziggy explained that this has been a very successful arrangement for both the inn and the co-eds. "They have a feeling of belonging," he said, "and we count on them to recommend people who they will enjoy working with."

Being a Cape Cod inn, naturally the menu has a great many seafood offerings including baked oysters, finnan haddie, and the Nantucket firemen's supper which is served on Wednesday nights. However, because of the Austrian influence there is also Viennese *tafelspitz,* Hungarian *gulyas,* and other continental specialities.

The big event every Tuesday evening is a clambake held in the garden of the inn, with lobsters, steamers, corn on the cob, melons, and all kinds of beverages. Hot dogs and hamburgers for the younger generation are also available for a very reasonable price. This is quite popular with the inn guests who live on the outer Cape.

Holidays are also something special. For example, on Thanksgiving, dinner is served family style and whole turkeys are proudly presented at each table. If desired, the head of the family can do the carving.

There's a pond down the road where guests can swim and a "house" beach where there's sand, surf, and waves. The outer Cape is a great place for bicycles.

"Is it fun to live in an inn?" I asked Sonja. "Oh yes," she replied enthusiastically. "I like to sweep the porch, change the flowers, and start the coffee machine in the morning. Daddy has also shown me how to put the muffins in the warmer and I can even answer the phone sometimes. Oh, here's our cat. Actually we have two cats — this one's called Minka, she has five toes."

"I see you've met our real innkeeper," Guenther remarked, as he joined us on the rear deck with some cups of aromatic coffee. "She's one of our greatest assets!"

Indeed, she is.

THE QUEEN ANNE INN, 70 Queen Anne Rd., Chatham, Mass. 02633; 617-945-0394. A 30-room village inn on Cape Cod on the picturesque south shore. Full American, modified American, or European plans. Open Easter thru Thanksgiving. Breakfast, dinner, Sunday brunch, and Tuesday clambake served to travelers. Near all of the Cape's scenic, cultural, and historical attractions. Water skiing, deep-sea fishing, sailing, bicycles, backroading, beach walking nearby. No recreational facilities for children on grounds. Nicole and Guenther Weinkopf, Innkeepers.

Directions: From Boston: Take Rte. 3 south to Sagamore Bridge crossing Cape Cod Canal. Continue on Rte. 6 to Exit 11; take Rte. 137 south to Rte. 28, turn left. This is Chatham's Main Street. Turn right into Queen Anne Rd. From New York: Take I-95 north to Providence, R.I.; I-195 to Wareham, and Rte. 6 to Sagamore Bridge (see directions above).

COBB'S COVE
Barnstable Village, Cape Cod, Massachusetts

Perhaps excerpts from this letter from a reader tells the story about Cobb's Cove most adroitly:

"After arriving too early, intruding upon their only chance of a private, lazy morning, Evelyn and Henri-Jean ushered me in, Annie Laurie at heel, and sat me down with coffee as if I were a long lost member of the family. The personal attention made all the difference and at Cobb's Cove I felt totally spoiled. 'Talk with us, make

yourself at home, browse through our selection of books (three walls full!). We'd love to see what you bought at the shops.'

"I asked myself, does one get this at the Hilton — I think not.

"There were many helpful and much appreciated suggestions of where to go, what to look for and what roads to take, plus a marked map to guide me through the late morning and early afternoon into a world I thought could only exist many more miles away than Cape Cod.

"I visited an incredible pottery shop and couldn't tear myself away until I purchased two delightful mirrors created by the craftsman's daughter. A few miles in the other direction I stood and watched open-mouthed as a very skilled lady wove a scarf in yellows, creams, and whites, her fingers moving so deftly over the ancient machine.

"The salt air seemed to beckon me closer so I parked the car, donned a quilted jacket and set off along the beach, matching my wits against the best of gulls as we battled the wind together, they making less headway than I. It was almost as if they were suspended from the clouds by an invisible thread.

"Back in the comfort of my room at Cobb's Cove, I felt warm and protected and yet at the same time aware of the gusts that buffeted the house and in the distance, the pounding of the waves.

"The evening meal was a truly lovely affair. All the guests chatted their way through an incredible five-course dinner which brought utter joy to each taste bud. For the most part, Evelyn and Henri-Jean sat back and watched as the rest of the group discussed matters from English royalty to collecting sea-shells. More attentive hosts we couldn't have asked for — we wanted for nothing and enjoyed everything.

"When it came time to leave my legs seemed like lead. The thought of leaving my haven and heading back to reality didn't sit at all well and Henri-Jean and Evelyn made it no easier with their warm send-off. I'd begun to get too used to retiring at night with not a sound outside except the wind rustling the leaves; waking in the morning to the smell of fresh-perked coffee, homemade rolls and bacon wafting up the stairs to the room I'd come so easily to call 'mine.'

"What a wonderful weekend. I met some beautiful people and I'm happy to say I had the opportunity to exchange addresses and phone numbers with six of the guests. What a shame you couldn't have made a surprise visit, your name entered into our conversation more than once."

That must have been the weekend my ears were burning.

COBB'S COVE, Barnstable Village, Rte. 6A, Cape Cod, Ma. 02630; 617-362-9356. A 6-room secluded inn on Cape Cod's north shore. Lodgings include a full breakfast. Houseguests can arrange for dinner. Open every day in the year. Within a short distance of Cape Cod Bay and the Atlantic Ocean, the U.S. National Seashore, and Sandy Neck Conservatory, as well as many museums, art galleries, craft shops, and other attractions of the Cape. Active sports nearby. No facilities to amuse children at the inn. No pets. Credit cards not accepted. Evelyn Chester, Innkeeper.

Directions: From Rte. 6 (Mid-Cape Hwy.), turn left at Exit 6 on Rte. 132 to Barnstable. Turn right on Rte. 6A, approximately 3 mi. through Barnstable Village, past the only traffic light and turn left just past the Barnstable Unitarian Church. After approximately 300 yds., look for small wooden sign on left at a gravel driveway saying: "Evelyn Chester."

THE BRAMBLE INN GALLERY AND CAFE
Brewster, Massachusetts

There is not just *one* big piece of news from The Bramble Inn for 1982, but *two,* and both of them are most exciting.

First of all, innkeepers Karen Etsell and Elaine Brennan are the authors of a wonderful book entitled, *How to Open a Country Inn.*

The timing was perfect. For many years I've been receiving letters from readers and travelers using *CIBR* who wanted to have as much information as possible about opening a country inn. When Karen and Elaine first approached me with the idea, I knew that the time had come, and these were just the right people to prepare such a book. Published by the Berkshire Traveller Press, it is now available at bookstores all over North America, as well as at the

country inns featured in this book. It has received wonderful reviews in newspapers and magazines, but most of all it has gained the complete endorsement of fellow-innkeepers. Be sure to have your copy autographed when you visit the inn. It is on sale at The Bramble Inn gift shop along with their cookbook.

The second news is that Karen and Elaine have bought the attractive house next door to the present Bramble Inn and spent the winter (between personal appearances and interviews) completely refinishing the interior and furnishing five additional lodging rooms, two with private baths. The architecture is Greek Revival, as is that of the Bramble, and it is painted white with green shutters (naturally) and has loads of pink and white petunias in front.

I first visited Karen and Elaine in 1976 and reported in the 1977 edition that The Bramble Gallery and Cafe (hereafter known as The Bramble Inn) was a dandy. If ever an inn had individuality without a single trace of stereotype, it is The Bramble.

From the very beginning, I found this inn delightful. The basic colors are green and pink and there are green placemats and pink napkins held in place by flowered rosebud napkin rings. The walls and woodwork are sparkling white and the floorboards of differing widths have been refinished with a warm brown patina. There are lots of hanging plants and ivy to provide more accents of green.

However, the main decor of the first floor is provided by a collection of watercolors, oil paintings, lithographs, pastels, and wood lathe art. Also scattered among these art pieces are photographs taken by Elaine. These adornments are all for sale.

The menu at The Bramble Inn has changed considerably since that first visit in 1976. Now it has expanded and there are delicious hearty entrées, as well as lighter offerings. The baked filets of sole are stuffed with chopped shrimp and almonds and covered with a rich Mornay sauce. It is delicious from the first bite. Another popular menu offering that provides a full meal is the carbonnade de boeuf bourguignon which is tender chunks of beef marinated in Burgundy wine and spices and baked slowly with fresh mushrooms, carrots, turnips, and onions. It is served with a green salad and freshly baked bread. The menu also has two varieties of crêpes, the Bramble Inn quiche, and the famous Cape Cod Bramble, an old-fashioned delicacy of chopped raisins and cranberries gently sweetened and wrapped in a tender pastry and topped with vanilla ice cream. Wow! It now has a registered federal trademark.

So, with the publication of *How to Open a Country Inn,* acquisition of the building next door thereby adding five more lodging rooms, and the redecoration of the upper floor of the inn, the years 1981 and 1982 are most significant for Karen Etsell and Elaine Brennan, two enterprising women who have not only attained their dreams but have done so with unmistakable style and class.

THE BRAMBLE INN GALLERY AND CAFE, Route 6A, Main St., Brewster, Cape Cod, Ma. 02631; 617-896-7644. A 7-room village inn (two with private bath) and art gallery in the heart of one of Cape Cod's northshore villages. Lodgings include continental breakfast. Open May through Oct. Lunch and dinner served daily except Sundays from mid-June through Labor Day. Swimming, sailing, water sports, golf, recreational and natural attractions within a short drive. Adjacent to tennis club. This is a small, intimate inn and does not meet the needs of most children. No pets. Credit cards accepted for meals and purchase of art work. Personal checks for lodgings. Elaine Brennan and Karen Etsell, Innkeepers.

Directions: Take Exit 10 from Rte. 6. Follow the intersection of Rte. 6A (4 mi.). Turn right, one-tenth mile to inn.

THE RED INN
Provincetown, Massachusetts

On the map, Cape Cod looks like an arm flexed at the elbow with the fingers curling in. The Red Inn in Provincetown is located right at the tip of those curling fingers.

For twelve years this restaurant has been owned and operated by Ted and Marce Barker with assorted sons, daughters, brothers, uncles, aunts, and now a growing list of newer members by marriage.

What I'd like to share with everyone this time is an account of some of the activities at Thanksgiving and Christmas at this year-round inn. They illustrate the tender care and wholehearted concern that everyone at the Red Inn feels for their guests.

As Ted writes, "At Thanksgiving, the preparation begins many days ahead of time with the relishes, sauces (cranberries everywhere),

breads (oh, the breads!)—banana-nut, date-nut, and cranberry bread, too. The Hubbard squash has to be cooked at least a day ahead—a squash worth its salt has to be at least a day old in order to have achieved good full flavor. Marce's Aunt Honey traditionally makes the pumpkin, mince, and apple pies for our Thanksgiving 'groaning board.'

"Leading up to Christmas, it's a day-by-day process of decoration. There's a lot of advance planning. It all takes on a 'homemade' approach. Many years before they could be purchased in stores, Mother Barker made all of our calico wreaths, yarn dolls, and countless ornaments, including yarn tassels, antique bowls, pitchers, jugs, cream cans, milk cans, and baskets of all sizes and shapes. All of these, as if by some magic husbandry, begin to grow evergreen branches mixed with bittersweet and wild cranberries. There are bows of red, calico, and even plaid.

"As for Christmas trees, we now have three. There's a little tree at the front door festooned with our handmade yarn tassels. The next tree is full and bushy and very traditional, and stands in the corner of the Tavern Lounge by the fireplace. This is also our family tree under which Santa places all the presents. The third tree stands tallest in the greenhouse dining area, perhaps ten or twelve feet high.

"We are blessed with a large 'combined' family, as you know, but as we have grown we have added new members who have grown with us and shared the spirit necessary to operate a good country inn.

"Incidentally last winter, we moved some of the dining room tables into the Tavern Lounge room, up next to the fireplace, and served late lunch/early supper, and dinner there. It's a restaurant within a restaurant. Picture, if you will, the view of Provincetown

Harbor, calm or storm, dinner by candlelight, and a warm wood fire in the huge hearth! Shall I make a reservation?"

Yes indeed, Ted, you should certainly make a reservation, and I'm sure many people will visit Provincetown again in the winter and enjoy the fullness of the spirit of service at the Red Inn.

THE RED INN, 15 Commercial St., Provincetown, Mass. 02657; 617-487-0050. A waterside country restaurant with a striking view of Provincetown Harbor. No lodgings. Open for lunch and dinner every day of the year. During winter a late lunch/early dinner is offered. Within walking distance of all Provincetown lodging accommodations and recreational activities and attractions. Guided "whale-watching" excursions. Ted and Marcie Barker, Innkeepers.

Directions: Follow Rte. 6 to end of Cape Cod.

JARED COFFIN HOUSE
Nantucket Island, Massachusetts

I've been out to Nantucket a number of times. Each time I get the same wonderful twinge of anticipation driving from Falmouth to Woods Hole. There's a point where I can see the whole harbor and be reassured that either the ferry "Nebska" or the "Uncatena" has not left without me. I think this comes from having missed it on an earlier occasion.

On arriving in Nantucket by ferry, there's the game of picking out the landmarks as the boat makes its way into the breakwater and the dock. The high-spired churches, the waterfront buildings and towers gradually take form. Then, there is the fun of actually going across the gangplank and putting your foot right down smack on Nantucket Island, the same Nantucket where shipowner Jared Coffin built his house.

The Jared Coffin House is truly extraordinary. It was built in 1845 by one of the island's most successful shipowners. A number of years ago the buildings were restored to their original style both in architecture and furnishings. Today, the JC helps recapture the spirit and feeling of the glorious days of Nantucket's reign as queen of the world's whaling ports.

It's difficult to believe that this sturdily built, Federally dimensioned house is an inn. Only the discreet murmur of voices and muffled clinking of silver from a tree-shaded patio gives its identity away. It seems just like the other handsome houses of Nantucket whaling captains.

It was good to see Phil and Peggy Read again, and I was very pleased that I would again be spending my visit in the Crewel Room with those splendid four-poster beds and the beautiful antiques.

Interestingly enough, I have met three other people in my travels about the country who have been guests at the Jared Coffin House, and were also put in the Crewel Room.

In reviewing some of the events at the Coffin House in the last thirteen years, probably the most significant is that Peggy and Phil Read are now the sole proprietors, as well as the innkeepers of this classic country inn. In 1978, a beautiful 1821 Federal house on Center Street, across the street from the inn on the dining room side, was purchased and converted into additional lodgings with six lovely rooms decorated and furnished in keeping with the Federal style.

Nantucket was seriously damaged by the Great Fire of 1846, and the discovery of gold in California and the subsequent discovery of oil in Pennsylvania caused the depletion of the great whaling oil industry on Nantucket. These combined to isolate the island for many years.

Although Nantucket was known for years primarily as a summer resort, it has become more and more popular as an out-of-season resort as well. A visit early in the year will bring unusual glimpses of an early New England spring, while the fall months offer some of the most beautiful days, warm and clear, with vivid and unforgettable colorings of the moors. And Christmas at the Jared Coffin is really special.

I enjoy just strolling about the winding streets, happily coping with the cobblestones, and bicycling out to look at the Scotch heather, wood lilies, and wild roses on the moors. These also provide a haven for rare birds such as the Swedish nightingale and the yellow-bellied bulbul.

This kind of activity naturally makes for a hearty appetite, and I particularly favor the Jared Coffin specialties such as quahaug chowder and bay scallops. The menu is classical American cuisine for which the inn has received several awards and much recognition.

Visiting Nantucket is always a unique experience. Staying at the Jared Coffin House is probably the closest thing that I've found to actually feeling like I am a native for a few days.

JARED COFFIN HOUSE, Nantucket Island, Mass. 02554; 617-228-2400. A 46-room village inn 30 mi. at sea. European plan. Breakfast, lunch, dinner served daily (food service in Tap Room only in Jan., Feb., Mar.). Strongly advise verifying accommodations before planning a trip to Nantucket in any season. Swimming, fishing, boating, golf, tennis, riding, and bicycles nearby. Philip and Margaret Read, Innkeepers.

Directions: Accessible by air from Boston, New York, and Hyannis, or by ferry from Woods Hole and Hyannis, Mass. Automobile reservations are usually needed in advance: 617-540-2022. Cars are not recommended for short stays. Seasonal air service from New York and ferry service from Hyannis are available May thru October: 617-426-1855. Inn is located 300 yards from ferry dock.

CHARLOTTE INN
Edgartown, Martha's Vineyard, Massachusetts

Innkeeper Gery Conover and I were having lunch at the Chez Pierre, which is a French restaurant operated in conjunction with the Charlotte Inn. It had a kind of indoors-outdoors atmosphere with many, many plants arranged around the brick garden and with trees arching overhead. A discreet gate on South Summer Street separated us from the passersby, who were doing what so many people do in Edgartown—strolling and looking at the beautiful Federalist and Greek Revival houses.

Chez Pierre is noted as one of the top French restaurants on the island, to which visitors come from all over the Cape to dine. It's run by a young couple who take great pride in their cooking.

Besides the Chez Pierre, the first floor of the inn's main building is occupied by a five-room art gallery and a gift shop.

Gery's two sons, Gery, Jr., 19, and Timmy, 12, stopped off on their way to go sailing in the Edgartown Harbor. "Many of the inn guests find the harbor a very pleasant diversion," he remarked, "and they can rent different types of sailboats and power boats from the boat livery.

"We are open year-round. Good sailing days start early in the spring and extend through the fall. It's interesting, though, how

145

many people come out to visit us during the so-called off-season. Edgartown is delightful when it is more quiet and has fewer visitors. Our guests enjoy shopping in town, walking along the beaches, and biking down to Chilmark which is at the other end of the island. You can really work up a good appetite. It's beautiful here during the Christmas and New Year's holidays. All of the islanders are very proud of their home decorations."

Like many other Edgartown houses, the Charlotte Inn is a classic, three-story white clapboard with a widow's walk on top. It was the former home of a Martha's Vineyard sea captain. There have been some changes, but basically, the building is the same as it was during the days of Edgartown's whaling heyday.

Lodging rooms at this inn are individually furnished and great care has been exercised in their decoration. All the rooms are very quiet and have their own private baths, and guests may enjoy a continental breakfast served in their rooms. A warm feeling of hospitality and a romantic atmosphere greets each guest.

My large room had a working fireplace for guests to use in the winter, and was furnished with antiques, including a four-poster queen-sized bed. It had a pleasant view of the garden and courtyard. As in all the other rooms, there were fresh flowers, lots of books and magazines, good reading lamps, and candlewick bedspreads.

My visit included a complete tour of the old whaling home, which is immediately next door to the main inn, where Gery has now created several additional romantic bedrooms all in the style of those in the main house.

The Carriage House at the rear of the inn has been fully restored and gives the impression, both inside and out, of being at least a hundred years old. Two of the rooms have fireplaces.

Travel writer Horace Sutton speaks of the Charlotte Inn as one of the nation's handsomest and as being "a museum of art that takes boarders."

CHARLOTTE INN, So. Summer St., Edgartown, Martha's Vineyard Island, Ma. 02539; 617-627-4751. An 18-room combination inn-art gallery and restaurant located on one of the side streets in the village of Edgartown, just a few short steps from the harbor. European plan. Rooms available every day of the year. Continental breakfast served to inn guests. Chez Pierre restaurant open for lunch and dinner from mid-March through New Year's Day. Other island restaurants open year-round. Boating, swimming, beaches, fishing, tennis, riding, golf, sailing, and biking nearby. No pets. Gery Conover, Innkeeper.

Directions: Martha's Vineyard Island is located off the southwestern coast of Cape Cod. The Woods Hole-Vineyard Haven Ferry runs year-round and automobiles may be left in the parking lot at Woods Hole. Taxis may be obtained from Vineyard Haven to Edgartown (8 mi.). Check with inn for ferry schedules for all seasons of the year. Accessible by air from Boston and New York.

THE VILLAGE INN
Lenox, Massachusetts

Here's Amy Judd, assistant innkeeper, on what it's like at the Village Inn on a Sunday morning in October:

"My first reaction is that during foliage season it's very busy. There are lots of happy people here because they have usually stayed overnight and are enjoying breakfast with us. If I do say so, we do feed them very well and fully.

"Breakfast can be anything from a bowl of cereal and a muffin to bacon and eggs, omelets, french toast, pancakes, and eggs Benedict with champagne. We serve it until one o'clock. At 11:30 guests can enjoy brunch or lunch."

Amy excused herself from the couch in front of the fireplace where we were chatting and ushered a group of people into the dining room which was now almost filled. The Village Inn has become a popular place for weekend breakfasts, not only for houseguests but for people who are visiting Lenox for the day. The lobby is a low-ceilinged room with flowered paper, old photographs and paintings, as well as a generous number of books. A big brass caldron of logs supplies the fire and there is an old-fashioned bellows.

Amy rejoined me, and I asked her what was the most exciting thing about keeping an inn.

"As you know I'm interested in the theater," she responded,

"and appear in many productions here in the Berkshires. Many innkeepers say that running an inn is like putting on a show and the first act really starts at the front desk when guests come in. If the first impression is a good one then they're happy from that point on. I think Act I, Scene II takes place when they see their room and I must say that our rooms are all lovingly decorated and kept in the colonial flavor of the building which couldn't take any other style. They all have low ceilings and copies of colonial wallpaper."

Amy and I continued to draw the parallel between a play and an inn, covering some of the luncheon menu which included crêpes, overstuffed sandwiches, scrod, and homemade soup, as well as special desserts. We decided that the final scene was probably a pleasant night's rest, and perhaps the after-piece takes place next morning as newfound friends regretfully say goodbye.

This particular scene was played many times during our conversation, as some lucky guests who were going to stay an extra day were off for a walk through the village and countryside, and others made their farewells.

The owners of the Village Inn are Cliff Rudisill and Ray Wilson, two interesting men with varied backgrounds. I enjoyed a very pleasant evening with them shortly before this book went to press at which time they explained that they are going to be serving afternoon tea every day, as well as dinners. During the summer the inn will offer light fare for enjoyment after the Boston Symphony Orchestra concerts at Tanglewood.

THE VILLAGE INN, Church St., Lenox, Mass. 01240; 413-637-0020. A 25-room inn in a bustling Berkshire town 4 mi. from Stockbridge, 8 mi. from Pittsfield, and 1 mi. from Tanglewood.

Lenox is located in the heart of the Berkshires with many historical, cultural, and recreational features. Breakfast, lunch, and dinner served daily to travelers. Open every day of the year, except Christmas Day. Swimming in pleasant nearby lakes. All seasonal sports including xc and downhill skiing available nearby. No pets. Personal checks accepted. Cliff Rudisill and Ray Wilson, Innkeepers.

Directions: After approaching Lenox on Rte. 7, one of the principal north-south routes in New England, exit onto Rte. 7A to reach the village center and Church Street. When approaching from the Mass Tpke. (Exit 2) use Rte. 20N about 4 mi. and turn left onto Rte. 183 to center of town.

THE INN AT HUNTINGTON
Huntington, Massachusetts

It was a beautiful, wintry Saturday night, just a day or two after the first snowfall in western Massachusetts, when once again I followed Route 20 from Lee up over Jacob's Ladder and down through the village of Chester to Huntington for my annual visit with Murray and Barbara Schuman at The Inn at Huntington.

The inn was decorated for Christmas with white candles in each of the windows and fresh Christmas garlands and other decorations in the dining rooms.

Murray, resplendent in his high chef's hat and cordial smile, greeted me in the hallway and sat for just a moment before it was necessary for him to return to the kitchen. "Tomorrow is the first day of our Russian Folk Christmas Feast," he said. "You know, we've done something different each Christmas for the last few years and Barbara and I have had a wonderful time creating a menu that includes many traditional Russian dishes. Each evening we have musicians presenting a recital of Russian music, and guests are invited to form a chorus of carolers at the conclusion of the feast."

Murray excused himself, but joined me for after-dinner coffee in the little sitting room in front of a lovely fire. Because I could hear the Vivaldi playing in the background and because I know of the Schumans' interest in both music and cuisine, I asked him if he had ever made any connection between the two.

"It's interesting that you should ask that," he said, settling back and stirring his coffee. "Eighteen years ago when I was first interested in cooking, it occurred to me that putting a meal together was probably similar to the way a musical director at Tanglewood would put a program together. You don't want all the same flavor, some variation is needed, and when the climax has come and gone, you want the listeners to leave feeling refreshed by the whole

149

experience. Oddly enough, I picked up a copy of the *Berkshire Eagle* and read a statement by Eric Leinsdorf to the effect that when he puts a musical program together he does it in much the same way a chef would put a menu together!"

He continued, "First there is something light, musically it captures the interest and the mood, and here at the inn it's an hors d'oeuvre plate, a medley of marinated fresh vegetables where colors are of prime importance as well the shapes and the seasonings. The soup would normally come next; it's an overture. This would be followed by something lighter, a way of clearing your palate. In music it would be one of the movements of a symphony; for dinner it would be a salad.

"The main dish, of course, corresponds to the principal work of the program and the dessert would be the encore. This is meant to recall all of the flavors and to say, 'this has been fun and tasty, and now we have something light and frivolous.'"

He threw another log on the fire, saying, "By the way, we do have bedrooms available now, but only by advance arrangements. They are usually rented to whole groups, but are also available to individuals as well."

He also explained that Barbara's *Cookery Bookery,* a unique catalogue which combines her love of books with the knowledge gained in the specialized field of cooking and gastronomy, was doing very well. This catalogue is available by mail and lists many rare and valuable out-of-print cookbooks.

"Our fresh pasta restaurant in Northampton, the Andiamo, is also thriving," Murray added.

On my return journey I pondered some of Murray's statements about the similarities between creating a dinner menu and a musical program. It occurred to me that for these past few years, not only have I always enjoyed a wonderful dinner at The Inn at Huntington, but it has also been a stimulating experience in other ways as well.

THE INN AT HUNTINGTON, Worthington Rd., Huntington, Ma. 01050; 413-667-8868. A restaurant featuring European country-side cuisine on Rte. 112 (Worthington Rd.) 1 mi. from downtown Huntington. Lodgings available by advance arrangements. Dinner served Wed. thru Sun., from Mar. 5 to Dec. 31. Reservations strongly suggested. Sun. aft. concerts during spring and fall; call for schedule. Closed Thanksgiving, Christmas Eve, Christmas Day. No credit cards. Murray and Barbara Schuman, Innkeepers.

Directions: Huntington is on Rte. 112, off U.S. Rte. 20, halfway between the Westfield and Lee exits of the Mass. Tpke. From Northampton use Rte. 66 to Rte. 112 to Huntington.

MORRILL PLACE
Newburyport, Massachusetts

The scene bordered on the idyllic. I was on the screened-in summer porch of the Morrill Place with Monroe purring contentedly on the wicker couch beside me while we both watched Buns, the resident bunny rabbit, eating the nasturtiums in the window box. Innkeeper Rose Ann Hunter was reading to me from John P. Marquand's account of Newburyport. "Newburyport appears at its best," she read, "on a clear October day, for October is usually the most genial month in northeastern Massachusetts. Our October skies are clear and soft blue. Such leaves as are left on the elms are an unobtrusive russet yellow.

"In October, you will find that Newburyport still offers an illusion of security, a blending of past and present, and the serene sort of disregard for the future that is one of the greatest charms of an old New England seaport.

"Newburyport is not a museum piece, although it sometimes looks it. It has some of the most perfect examples of early Colonial and Federal architecture in America, but it is a vital, tolerant place and still able to keep up with the times, if you get to know it."

I was seeing Newburyport through the eyes of this very enthusiastic young woman who moved here a few years ago. In addition to having shown me through the graceful Newburyport mansion which has been turned into a warm and receptive guest house, she was kind enough to take me on a comprehensive tour of the town and the Parker River National Wildlife Refuge on Plum Island.

"Morrill Place was built in 1806," Rose Ann said, "by Kathyrn and William Hoyt. The owners include three Newburyport sea captains—that's why there's a widow's walk. We have fourteen guest rooms and we are always open, even through the holidays. There are twelve working fireplaces."

We were joined for a moment by Kristen, who is an energetic seven-year-old.

Earlier in the afternoon, my house tour started at the front of the house in the formal living room which is adorned with oriental *objets d'art*. I marveled at the double-hung staircase with the six-inch risers. "This was built at the time when women wore hoop skirts," Rose Ann explained. "Double-hung staircases are rare, even in Newburyport."

Many of the bedrooms have fireplaces and were being redecorated with distinctive period wallpapers. I saw my first "Indian shutters" which, when closed, left a narrow horizontal open slit. "In the 18th century, the real danger was from marauding pirates," she explained.

My room was named after Daniel Webster who was a frequent visitor to the house. There was a remarkably preserved print of Mr. Webster over the fireplace, and the furnishings were typical of other bedrooms, including an antique deacons' bench, two twin beds, each embellished with a pineapple motif, a lovely old chest of drawers, and a Boston rocker.

Our tour, as so many do, ended up in the kitchen where we had a refreshing cup of tea and I learned that the breakfasts include juice, coffee or tea, cereal, fresh baked rolls and English muffins, topped off by "mother's strawberry jam."

How could I help but like the Morrill Place with a cat named Monroe and a rabbit named Buns?

MORRILL PLACE, 209 High St., Newburyport, Ma. 01950. (617-462-2808.) A 14-room guest house on one of Newburyport's beautiful, residential avenues. Most rooms share bath with one other room. Lodgings include continental breakfast, only meal offered. Open every day in year. Within a very convenient distance of all of the Newburyport historical and cultural attractions, and Plum Island Wildlife Refuge. Other recreational facilities nearby. Rose Ann Hunter, Innkeeper.

Directions: From Boston follow I-95 north and take Historic Newburyport exit and follow Rte. 113. This becomes High St. Follow it for about 2 miles. Inn is on right hand side at corner of Johnson and High St. From Maine: Exit I-95 for Historic Newburyport and follow above directions.

WINDSOR HOUSE
Newburyport, Massachusetts

"Actually," said Judith Crumb, putting a rather English flavor into her diction, "We are offering two different types of dinner here at the inn. The first is Supper With the Innkeeper, a rather informal affair served in the kitchen, and Fritz and I eat with the guests. There's usually a four- or five-course meal and unless there are dietary restrictions it's chef's choice. It gives Fritz a great forum to try out new dishes or repeat family favorites, and he often gives cooking hints as he adds the final touches.

"Our Edwardian Feasts are truly regal occasions. We suggest formal attire, we all wear evening clothes and there is court music playing in the background. The Feast itself starts at 7:30 and consists of at least ten courses—fish, poultry, and meat courses are mixed with aspics and savories and sweets.

"We only accept reservations for one type of dinner per day and so they should be made well in advance. We can feed up to six guests for Supper with the Innkeeper and we can seat from two to six for the Edwardian Feast, but we accept only one party. Menus are submitted if the guest requests."

The Windsor House was built in 1796 as both a residence and a ship's chandlery office. The kitchen was the original shipping and receiving room, as can be seen from the big outside doors. There are a series of trapdoors which go up to the fourth story of the house where there is a huge iron hoist wheel.

The brick wall of the fireplace is a part of a fire wall that extends to the top story and separates the old warehouse section

from the living section. The posts and beams throughout the entire house were built by ships' carpenters.

The kitchen is really the pulse of the Windsor House. Not only do the guests gather around in the morning to enjoy Fritz's preprandial skills, but as Judith says, "It's the place where we all gather *any* time during the day and tell tales and get acquainted."

Guests at the inn continually write me complimentary notes about the breakfast that is included with the room tariff. Judith speaks of it as "a proper two-course English breakfast," although she points out that unlike the Britons, "Our toast is served warm instead of cold. Most breads are baked in the kitchen and there is a traditional English breakfast cake and English County Fair egg bread which is particularly yummy. Fritz has several culinary inspirations at breakfast time including a Rink Tum Tidy or Nantucket soufflé. There are lots of herbed eggs and each order is cooked to the guest's preference."

Three of the lodging rooms have private baths and three have shared baths. There are two family-suite combinations available, and trundle beds for small people. One of these suites has its own entrance at the street level and is ideal for elders or guests who might find stairs a problem.

On the very top floor it is possible to look out of the bedroom windows and see the houses that survived the Newburyport fire of 1811.

Part and parcel of any guest's stay is the rather unique collection of house pets including Sir Thomas More and Erasmus of Rotterdam, two very friendly cats. The newest addition is Merlin, a very young feline who is growing all the time. Lilabet, the toy poodle, is there to greet guests as they arrive and even, so it is said, tries to take telephone messages.

The Windsor House is within a pleasant stroll of the fascinating Newburyport waterfront.

WINDSOR HOUSE, 38 Federal Street, Newburyport, Ma. 01950; 617-462-3778. A 6-room inn located in the restored section of Newburyport. Open year-round. Breakfast served to all guests; dinner by 3-day advance reservation. Three miles from the Merrimack River Valley, Plum Island, and the Parker River National Wildlife Refuge. A short walk from the restored 19th-century retail area, restaurants, and museums. Also nearby: deep sea fishing, swimming, art galleries, antique shops, family ski area, horseback riding, and year-round theater. Some trundle beds available for children; no cribs or playpens. Parents must provide for infant care. Small dogs welcome. Can meet bus or planes at local airport.

Directions: From Boston and Maine: From I-95 use Exit to Rte. 113, turn right onto High St. (Rte. 1A) and proceed three miles to Federal St., turn left. Inn on left across from Old South Church (Rte. 1A is scenic drive from either Boston or New Hampshire).

NAUSET HOUSE INN
East Orleans, Massachusetts

"They thought we were crazy when we bought this glass greenhouse and had it shipped from Greenwich," said Jack Schwarz as we sat in the comfortable confines of this most unusual addition to the Nauset House Inn. "It was buit in 1908 on a Connecticut estate and it arrived here in a totally dismantled state. It had to be carefully and painstakingly reassembled. Of course our guests talk about it all the time. Some of them refer to it as our 'giant erector set.'"

Well, all kidding aside, the conservatory (I think that's the best name for it) is really a smash hit at this little inn which is located about three-quarters of the way out to the end of Cape Cod. It is used from opening day in April until mid-November. It is pleasant in early spring and late autumn, and even on some of the warmer days of summer it is quite comfortable, thanks to the ocean breeze that wafts through the louvered roof.

Lucille Schwarz, bearing a fresh cup of steaming coffee, joined us and I asked her what it feels like here in the conservatory in April. "Oh," she replied enthusiastically, "the geraniums are in full bloom

and the camellias do very well here. We keep them in the main house most of the winter along with some of the tropical plants and flowers. In April everything is brought out here including the rhododendrons, and with the help of the wonderful sunshine we push spring up at least thirty days.

"We had two weddings in April and May and I'm delighted to say that we had a total of eight weddings during the entire year. The couples take their vows in front of our dolphin fountain and the reception is held in the dining room."

Jack, not to be outdone, remarked, "We also had two pre-1950 jazz sessions here. Cape Cod apparently is the home of many retired musicians of the big-band era who are readily available for an afternoon or early evening session."

Let me hasten to explain that the inn itself is in a venerable old building of colonial design, and since Jack and Lucy are also in the business of buying and selling antiques, all of the lodging rooms have been furnished with an extensive collection of handsome beds, chests, clocks, highboys, and other early American antiques. Bathrooms are small and spotless and the view from the upstairs room is across the fields to the beach. Everything is cozily situated in an apple orchard.

The beach is famous Nauset Beach with some of the best surf in New England. It's also an ideal place for jogging because there are ten miles of empty seashore at low tide. Guests obtain a pass from the inn because it is not a public beach.

Breakfast is the only meal served at the inn and there is something different every day, for example quiche Lorraine or cranberry muffins or sour cream coffee cake or french toast. The maple syrup is right from the Schwarz's farm in Vermont.

Lucille excused herself, and Jack and I wandered out past the swimming pool into the orchard. "It's a very interesting point," he said, "that over three-quarters of our fall guests were from west of the Mississippi River. Most were from California, many from Ohio, Illinois, and Texas, and eight from Minnesota. Eleven of our couples in the autumn came from Europe."

Personally I prefer to travel on Cape Cod in the fall because the weather is gorgeous, it is still possible to take a dip in the ocean at noonday, and the backroading is always uncrowded.

NAUSET HOUSE INN, P.O. Box 446, Nauset Beach Rd., East Orleans, Cape Cod, Mass. 02643; 617-255-2195. A 12-room country inn 90 mi. from Boston, 27 mi. from Hyannis. Breakfast served to inn guests only. No other meals served. Some rooms with shared bath. Open daily from April 1 to Nov. 15. Within walking distance of Nauset Beach. Riding and bicycles nearby. No children under 12 yrs. No pets. Jack and Lucy Schwarz, Innkeepers.

Directions: From the Mid-Cape Hwy. (Rte. 6), take Exit 12. Bear right to first traffic light. Follow signs for Nauset Beach. Inn is located ¼ mi. before beach on Nauset Beach Rd.

Rhode Island

INN AT CASTLE HILL
Newport, Rhode Island

I was enjoying a few moments of quiet on the porch of one of the harbor houses at the Inn at Castle Hill watching the water traffic on Narragansett Bay. In the foreground, a young fisherman wearing very high orange boots was taking in his nets, and in the middle distance I counted at least seventeen sailboats, including one of the famous twelve-meter yachts that are used in the America's Cup Races. In the far distance there was the presence of the famous Newport Bridge which soars over the bay to Jamestown.

Coming up from the private beach below me was an attractive girl who replied that the water was "just perfect" to my question about the temperature.

It was early July, and I was visiting my good friend Paul McEnroe whom I have known ever since the late '60s when he was the innkeeper at the de la Vergne Farms Inn in Amenia, New York. Paul has been here in Newport for a number of years and we both remarked on how different the atmosphere was from his home state.

Each one of the harbor houses is beautifully furnished with its own bathroom and is roomy enough to accommodate three people comfortably. All of them were newly decorated and the bright white walls and gay curtains and bedspreads were just perfect for the waterside atmosphere.

In addition to these lodgings, there are several rooms in the main mansion of the Inn at Castle Hill. This was once the property of the eminent naturalist Alexander Agassiz who built Castle Hill one hundred years ago as a summer residence. It has remained unchanged in character and many of the original furnishings, including oriental rugs and the handcrafted oak and mahogany paneling, are still intact. "This was all done before Newport really became a chic society hideout," said Paul. "Agassiz built this mansion for himself and it really was one of the forerunners of Newport's later resplendence."

Paul and I strolled along the grassy bank to the deck of the main house where luncheon was served in full view of the ever-changing panorama of sea, sky, and ships. The menu included several very enticing offerings including a variety of omelets, crêpes, quiches, and salads.

Our conversation naturally led to the dinners at the inn, and Paul explained that the inn takes a limited number of diners each night and "they must be spaced just right. Dinner takes from two to two-and-a-half hours, so we naturally cater to people who are not in a hurry. Our dinners are now 98 per cent by reservation, and we only hold a table ten minutes. We always request that they not be late in order to avoid any misunderstandings.

The evening mean is oriented to French cuisine and includes hot and cold hors d'oeuvres, soups, salads, and fish, fowl, lamb, veal, and beef, all cooked and served in the continental manner.

The European flavor of the Inn at Castle Hill is considerably reinforced by the road which leads from Ocean Drive through a small section of woods. It reminds me of the Barbizon Forest, about two hours south of Paris, which inspired a school of French painters, including Millet. When I remarked to Paul about this resemblence to inns I have visited in Europe, he responded enthusiastically, "That's exactly what we've tried to achieve. After all, this inn was built as a mansion and we're trying to recreate the elegance of Newport's past by having a menu, service, and furnishings that best suit our ideals. Jackets are required for dinner and no jeans, not even designer style, are allowed in the dining rooms. I'm sure that's the way it was eighty years ago."

Our regular readers will note that the dining rooms are now closed from January 3rd to Easter. However, rooms are available all winter with continental breakfast being served. The Sunday brunch is served from one o'clock to five in the afternoon from Easter through New Year's Day. Lunch and brunch are served on the outside deck during the summer months. There is Dixieland jazz on Sunday afternoons, and entertainment in the lounge.

INN AT CASTLE HILL, Ocean Drive, Newport, R.I. 02840; 401-849-3800. A 20-room mansion-inn on the edge of Narragansett Bay. European plan. Continental breakfast served to houseguests only. Lunch and dinner served daily to travelers. Dining room closed from Jan. 3 to Easter. Guest rooms open all winter. Lounge open winter weekends. Near the Newport mansions, Touro Synagogue, the Newport Casino, and National Lawn Tennis Hall of Fame, the Old Stone Mill, the Newport Historical Society House. Swimming, sailing, scuba diving, walking on grounds. Bicycles and guided tours of Newport nearby. No pets. Paul Goldblatt, Manager. Paul McEnroe, Innkeeper.

Directions: After leaving Newport Bridge follow Bellevue Ave. which becomes Ocean Dr. Look for inn sign on left.

LARCHWOOD INN
Wakefield, Rhode Island

The Larchwood is a large mansion in the village of Wakefield, dating back to 1831, set in the middle of a large parklike atmosphere with copper, beech, ginkgo, pin oak, spruce, mountain ash, maple, Japanese cherry trees, evergreens, dogwoods, and a very old mulberry tree. In all there are three acres of trees and lawn.

The interior has many Scottish touches, including quotations from Robert Burns and Sir Walter Scott, and photographs and prints of Scottish historical and literary figures. One of the dining rooms has murals showing farms and seascapes of southern Rhode Island. On a recent trip I discovered a little sign I'd never seen before that said: "The Larchwood Inn where innkeeping is still in keeping." I detected a touch of innkeeper Frank Browning's sense of humor.

We were all in good humor that evening at dinner which began with an experience I've never had at any other inn. The waiter brought in a large silver tray with a choice of at least *four* different salads. "This has proven to be something that our guests enjoy very much," said Frank with a broad smile. "You're always talking about doing something 'memorable' and I think this fills the bill."

Since it was midsummer and real ocean weather, the conversation turned to the many beaches that are found throughout southern Rhode Island. "Most of these beaches are available without any permits," explained Frank. "Our houseguests frequently return on sunny afternoons with bright sunburns and stories about beaches they're sure no one else has discovered.

"One of the interesting parts of our summer dinner business is from people that are cruising on their boats. Our inn is about a mile and a half from Ram Point Marina which is at the head of Point Judith Pond. It is the largest and best facility in the area. We frequently get calls from people at the marina asking for reservations and directions. We often transport them back to their boat."

160

Because of the Scottish heritage which dates back to the previous owners, Mr. and Mrs. Hugh Cameron, Robert Burns's birthday is one of the big nights at the Larchwood Inn. "It's more popular than New Year's Eve," Frank remarked. "We're always booked six weeks in advance and we have a professional piper for the evening, a gentleman named John Alder who piped in the Queen of England at Newport a few years ago."

While I was looking at the menu Frank pointed out that a new feature was a lighter supper which included quiche Lorraine and quiche with crab, as well as various types of omelets and hot prime ribs of beef or sliced turkey sandwiches. "We're serving these in addition to our regular dinners," he said, "because many people would like something a little lighter or they come in later after a party. Of course we still have shrimp, lobster, swordfish, scallops, and langostinos."

After dinner, which was topped off with a Larchwood Inn "special"—an almond-flavored chiffon pie covered with whipped cream and grated chocolate—we took a walk through the grounds and Frank reminisced about some of his early days at the inn in 1946 when he was just a kitchen boy. Now he is both the owner and the innkeeper. We were joined by his golden retriever who answered to the name of Drake.

By the way, the Larchwood Inn is a few miles from Point Judith, Rhode Island, where the ferry leaves for Block Island. The Larchwood makes a nice overnight stop.

LARCHWOOD INN, 176 Main St., Wakefield, R.I. 02879; 401-783-5454. An 11-room village inn just 3 mi. from the famous southern R.I. beaches. Some rooms with shared bath. European plan. Breakfast, lunch, dinner served every day of the year. Swimming, boating, surfing, fishing, xc skiing, and bicycles nearby. Francis Browning, Innkeeper.

Directions: From Rte. 1, take Pond St. Exit and proceed ½ mi. directly to inn.

THE INNTOWNE
Newport, Rhode Island

During the more than seventeen years I've been making an annual project out of rewriting this book, there have been a number of interesting innovations and permutations among the many innkeepers with whom I've become acquainted.

Paul and Betty McEnroe are a case in point. I first met them in 1965 when they were innkeepers at the De la Vergne Farms Inn in Amenia, New York, which was included in the very first edition of *CIBR*. They, in turn, told me about Rodney and Ione Williams and the Inn at Sawmill Farm, which has been one of my regular visiting places since the late '60s.

The inn in Amenia was unfortunately destroyed by fire, and Paul and Betty relocated in Newport as the innkeepers of the Inn at Castle Hill. Meanwhile, being both creative and enterprising, they recognized the possibilities in converting a dilapidated old brick building of some architectural integrity in downtown Newport into an inn. It was quite natural for them to turn to Rodney and Ione, who are extremely well-known designers and decorators, to help with the project.

The result is an elegant Colonial inn in the heart of historic Newport which, like the Inn at Sawmill Farm, is a model for country inn decor and ambience.

"Ione was really involved in choosing all of the draperies, bedspreads, and wallpaper, even to the harmonizing colors in the lampshades," explained Betty McEnroe. "She carefully 'choreographed' — I think that's the best word for it — each room according to its size and the placement of the windows. We all agreed we wanted to achieve a feeling of lightheartedness and gaiety, but in a Colonial setting."

The lobby-living room area has some handsome antiques including an old grandfather's clock in a beautiful inlaid antique case, and one wall is a bookcase decorated with ivy plantings and a beautiful model ship. It's like being in a living room of a very elegant house of two hundred years ago.

The Inntowne is a perfect complement to the rest of historic

Bowen's Wharf

Newport. It is open twelve months of the year and it's most convenient for visiting Bowen's wharf with its many shops and boutiques. Furthermore, it's easy to drive around the city for a tour of the many mansions, some of which, along with the Tennis Hall of Fame, are open year around.

Betty and Paul serve continental breakfast in the engaging atmosphere of a little antique shop. As Betty says, "Our guests can enjoy the homemade muffins, juice, and coffee and then can purchase the bone china cup and saucer, the chair they sat on, the table they ate on, the oriental rug from the floor, or portraits from the wall."

The Inntowne does not accept reservations by mail, so please telephone only between the hours of 9:00 a.m. and 5:00 p.m. A tentative reservation can be made awaiting confirmation with deposit.

THE INNTOWNE, 6 Mary St., Newport, R.I. 02840; 401-846-9200. An elegant 20-room inn in the center of the city of Newport overlooking the harbor, serving continental breakfast only. Open every day. Reservations by telephone only between 9 a.m. and 5 p.m. Convenient for all of the Newport historical and cultural attractions which are extremely numerous. No recreational facilities available; however, tennis and ocean swimming are nearby. No pets. Not adaptable for children of any age. Betty and Paul McEnroe, Innkeepers.

Directions: After crossing Newport bridge turn right at sign: "Historic Newport." Drive straight to Thames Street; Inntowne is on corner of Thames St. and Mary St., across from Brick Marketplace.

THE 1661 INN
Block Island, Rhode Island

I read a most interesting article in the January 1981 edition of *Yankee* Magazine written by Dennis Lopez about being on Block Island in the winter. Thanks to some of his excellent color photography the article was made even more intriguing.

Mr. Lopez speaks enthusiastically about the winter storms and the fact that all of the year-round residents of the island know each other and there is a great sense of belonging to one great family. The photographs and text speak glowingly of winter days and skies on this island off the coast of southern New England.

What makes all of this more interesting is the fact that while the 1661 Inn is best-known for being a delightful retreat in three seasons of the year, portions of it are open year-round, and a winter holiday on the island sounds like a wonderful idea.

Rita Draper, the daughter of Joan and Justin Abrams, put it this way: "My husband Steve, our son Kyle, and I have been living at the inn's Guest House where there are eleven rooms with private baths, most of them with a water view. Steve and I will be providing a super continental breakfast and there are lots of really enjoyable things to do here during the winter including bicycling, beach walking, backroading, and just loafing about and reading. It's really quite romantic.

"Some provision is made for the evening meal—either I'll cook it or we'll recommend the places on the island that are really good. Your readers should call ahead. I'll also provide them with the daily ferry schedule."

It was a far cry from a Block Island winter on the July day of my last visit when Joan and Rita took me in tow, proudly displaying all of the redecorated rooms in the main inn and also the great progress at the Manisses, which is an old, almost-abandoned hotel whose salad days were at the turn of the century. The Abrams family, ever eager for challenge, decided to do it over, step-by-step and floor-by-floor. Restoration on the upper floors was nearly completed, and Joan showed me samples of Victorian wallpaper and Victorian furniture and rugs. "We've even been able to find 1870 chandeliers and old gas sconces that could be converted to electric," she said. "All the rooms will have private baths and some will have Jacuzzis. Everything ought to be ready by the first of May.

"We do not serve dinner at the inn anymore; however, many of the inn specialties are available for dinner at the Manisses."

Buffet breakfasts at the inn during the summer include fresh fruit salad, scrambled eggs, corned beef hash, quiche, roasted potatoes, and at least one or two other special dishes, such as chicken tetrazzini and vegetable casseroles, along with homemade muffins, breads, and jams. Guests eat either inside or at umbrella-topped tables out on the dining deck.

The late afternoon get-acquainted party at the inn features some of Joan's and Rita's rather special snacks.

So, it appears that the 1661 Inn is now an inn for all four seasons.

THE 1661 INN, Box 367, Block Island, R.I. 02807; 401-466-2421 or 2063. A 25-room island inn off the coast of R.I. and Conn. in Block Island Sound; 11 private baths. Open from Memorial Day thru Columbus Day weekend. Breakfast served to travelers daily. (Guest House open year-round; continental breakfast included in off-season rates; dinner upon request.) Lawn games on grounds. Tennis, bicycling, ocean swimming, sailing, snorkeling, diving, salt and fresh water fishing nearby. Block Island is known as one of the best bird observation areas on the Atlantic flyway. The Abrams Family, Innkeepers.

Directions: By ferry from Providence, Pt. Judith, and Newport, R.I. and New London, Ct. Car reservations must be made in advance for ferry. By air from Newport, Westerly, and Providence, R.I., New London and Waterford, Ct., or by chartered plane. Contact inn for schedules.

Connecticut

WHITE HART INN
Salisbury, Connecticut

"Northwestern Connecticut has names like Litchfield, Kent, Cornwall Bridge, Sharon, and Salisbury. There are winding roads, picket fences, old Colonials, horses, high hedges, and an appreciation for fine leathers and imported tweeds. The village of Salisbury sums it all up very nicely, and plump in the middle of it is the White Hart Inn, and the adjoining Country Store.

"There was a memorable day about six months ago when I held a five-minute conversation with the wooden Indian at the entrance of this Contry Store, thinking it was Innkeeper John Harney (there is a resemblance).

"John says of the White Hart Inn, 'We're as New England as Mom's apple pie.' He ought to know. Unlike Ethan Allen, the hero of Fort Ticonderoga who went from Salisbury to Vermont, John went the other way—from Vermont to Salisbury.

"The White Hart is a rambling old place with many fireplaces and chimney corners. The guest rooms are big and comfortable, and the food is plentiful. Sunday night buffets bring out many of the interesting people who have migrated to both the Litchfield Hills and the Berkshires from the metropolitan area. A lot of them have had their first taste of real New England as a result of staying at the White Hart on an earlier weekend visit.

"The Country Store is a replica of a similar emporium of 75 years ago, and sells all of the gimcracks, candles, soaps, spices, penny candy, etc., that we have come to associate with the late 1890s. However, I noted that there are quite a few new gadgets that may well be considered gimcracks in another hundred years. I have always found it very difficult just to browse and not to buy."

The above paragraphs are what I wrote in 1968 on one of my very first visits to the White Hart Inn. Everything I wrote then is true today, the only difference being that the White Hart has since celebrated its 100th birthday, and John Harney insists that he has been there at least 110 years!

Over the past few years I have described John beating me at checkers (I'm sure he's honest but why does he win every time?), John beating me at darts (I know he practices on the side), and John giving me history lessons about the lost community called Dudleytown. I have described the gingerbread village which is on display at the inn during every Christmas season, and also John's successes and failures in the world of politics.

I should make a mention of the fact that John is true to his last by offering not only traditional New England country fare on the menu, but also continental dishes and an extensive oriental menu, including Peking duck, sweet and sour pork, hot spicy, tangy chicken ball, and Buddhist delight vegetables. As John says, "They are all hot, spicy dishes, but you can order without the hot."

For some years now, John has also been the chief blender and distributor of Sarum tea which is imported from many of the exotic countries of the world.

Just as John Harney and the White Hart are a tradition in northwest Connecticut, I guess one might say they are also a tradition in *Country Inns and Back Roads,* since they were both in the first edition in 1966!

WHITE HART INN, Salisbury, Conn. 06068; 203-435-2511. A 25-room village inn, 55 mi. west of Hartford. European plan. Breakfast, lunch, dinner served to travelers daily. Alpine and xc skiing, ski-jumping, golf, swimming nearby. John Harney, Innkeeper.

Directions: Exit the Taconic Pkwy. at Millbrook, N.Y. Proceed east on U.S. 44 to Salisbury. Inn is located at Jct. of U.S. 44 and 41.

CURTIS HOUSE
Woodbury, Connecticut

"Yes, since the inn opened in 1754, I believe we are the oldest inn in Connecticut." The speaker was redhaired Gary Hardisty, himself a lifelong resident of Woodbury and a member of a family that has operated the Curtis House since early 1950.

"There have been quite a few changes and alterations over the years, and many different owners. However, since four of them, all

167

unrelated, were named 'Curtis' I believe that this is an appropriate name."

The Curtis House by any name is a real country inn experience. I visited it on a chilly Saturday afternoon in January after a pleasant snowfall the night before. Everything combined to make it idyllically New England. The countryside was at its best in a white mantle, and the 18th-century homes and churches in the towns and villages in northwest Connecticut, gleamed in the bright sunshine.

The drive from the Massachusetts Berkshires (Woodbury is in the Connecticut Berkshires) took about ninety minutes and I was eagerly anticipating lunch. As I opened the old front door, the heavenly odors of hearty New England cooking wafted toward me.

I walked through a narrow hall past the stairway to the lodging rooms on two floors above, and entered the low-ceilinged, heavily beamed dining room. Waitresses were bustling about carrying trays laden with beef pot pie, Yankee pot roast, roast beef hash, and scallops. The room was filled with happy people, including quite a few families of students at the local prep schools. I was given a quiet table in the corner, and my visit to the Curtis House began in earnest.

My luncheon included a delicious fresh fruit and sherbet cup, hot muffins, and a beef pie. From the desserts I chose an apple crisp which was served with vanilla ice cream. I noticed that the dinner menu offered these things and much more, including sweetbreads, roast beef, and quite a few dishes such as broiled bluefish.

I was delighted to discover that there were eighteen lodging rooms in this old inn, many of them with canopied twin or double beds. Twelve of the rooms have private baths. There are four more modern rooms in the nearby Carriage House.

Later, I chatted with Gary Hardisty in the living room with the fireplace and wide floorboards. He pointed out that the large inn signs outside were the work of Wallace Nutting who included many of the Woodbury buildings in his book, *Connecticut the Beautiful*. Gary mentioned that Woodbury was one of the antiquing centers of New England and there were many, many antique shops on Routes 6 and 47. The Glebe House which was the birthplace of the American Episcopal Church is only a ten-minute walk from the inn.

Gary explained that as a rule dinner reservations are not accepted, with the exception of New Year's Eve, Mother's Day, Easter, and Thanksgiving.

I learned that almost everything on the extensive menu is prepared from scratch and the inn does all of its own baking. Those warm muffins at lunch really hit the spot.

After spending the remaining part of the afternoon browsing through the village, I left Woodbury and the Curtis House as the setting sun created great red and orange streaks over the snowy hills and the lights of the inn were already casting their warm beckoning glow. This is the way it's been for well over 200 years.

CURTIS HOUSE, Route 6 (Main St.), Woodbury, Conn., 06798; 203-263-2101. An 18-room village inn, 12 mi. from Waterbury. Open year-round. European plan. Lodgings include continental breakfast. Lunch and dinner served daily except Christmas. No pets. Lodgings not adaptable to young children. Antiquing, skiing, tennis, platform tennis, horseback riding nearby. The Hardisty Family, Innkeepers.

Directions: From N.Y. take Sawmill River Pkwy. to I-84. Take Exit 15 from I-84 in Southbury. Follow Rte. 6 north to Woodbury. From Hartford take I-84 to Exit 17, follow Rte. 64 to Woodbury.

SILVERMINE TAVERN
Norwalk, Connecticut

"Meet Miss Abigail," said Frank Whitman. "She's the only woman permitted by Connecticut law to stand within three feet of a bar."

I spoke courteously, but Miss Abigail just stood there in her crinoline and lace, looking inscrutable. The walls behind her and, in fact, in all of the dining rooms were covered with old farm implements and tools, as well as American primitive paintings.

Frank and I continued our tour of the Silvermine Tavern. "The Tavern was named for the town," he said. "That name, in turn, came from an old as-yet-unfounded rumor about a silver mine

discovered by an early settler. The old post office was here at the four corners."

We passed through two low-ceilinged sitting rooms brimming with antiques. There were fireplaces in each and one had an old clock with wooden works. Frank pointed out the beams from the original inn as well as the old-fashioned colonial hinges on the doorway. Some of the oil paintings of the colonial ladies and gentlemen looked rather forbidding.

I followed him up a winding staircase and found typical country inn bedrooms without television or telephones. These are also to be found in other buildings.

"You can imagine that we're quite popular with honeymooners," he said. "They like to wander the country roads and to feed the ducks and swans on the Mill Pond." There is a Country Store just across the street from the Tavern where the old counters and display tables have some very interesting adaptations of colonial skills and crafts. In the back room of the store, a museum has antique tools and gadgets and a fine collection of Currier and Ives prints.

The Tavern at various times has served as a country inn, a gentleman's country seat, and a town meeting place. It has a very large outdoor dining area overlooking the Silvermine River and the Mill Pond with ducks and swans. Summer terrace dining among the oaks, maples, pines, and poplar trees is very popular with playgoers to the Westport Playhouse and the Stratford Shakespeare Theatre nearby. I like the Silvermine in the winter also, when the many fireplaces are crackling and the candles create a romantic feeling.

Some of the New England dishes on the menu include Indian

pudding, bread pudding, honeybuns, native scrod, lobster, scallops, and oysters. On Thursday night there is a buffet that includes roast beef, corned beef, and fried chicken. On Wednesday and Friday night during the summer there is a barbecue, and there is a Sunday brunch buffet which has as many as 25 different offerings on the big tables.

When my tour of the Tavern and all the buildings at the Crossroads was over, I went back to ask Miss Abigail if she'd care to join me for dinner. I suggested the chicken pie. No reply. I pointed out that all the breads and desserts were homemade—even the ice cream. Still she remained inscrutable.

But I didn't feel too badly when Frank assured me that she hasn't spoken to anyone in years.

SILVERMINE TAVERN, Perry Ave., Norwalk, Ct. 06850; 203-847-4558. A 10-room country inn in the residential section of Norwalk. Long Island Sound and beaches 6 mi. away. European plan includes continental breakfast. Lunch and dinner served to travelers daily. Open year-round. Closed Christmas Day and Tuesdays during winter. Golf, tennis, and fishing nearby. Francis C. Whitman, Innkeeper.

Directions: From New York or New Haven via I-95, take Exit 15. Pick up the new Rte. 7 going north. At the end of Rte. 7 (approx. 1 mi.) turn right, go to first stoplight, turn right. At next stoplight by firehouse turn right onto Silvermine Ave. Proceed down Silvermine Ave. about 2 mi. to Tavern. From I-84 and Danbury take old Rte. 7 south to Norwalk. Watch for Kelly Greens ½ mi. south of Merritt Pkwy. on the left, turn right on Perry Ave. opposite Kelly Greens. Follow Perry Ave. 2 mi. to Tavern. From Merritt Pkwy. take Exit 39 south on old Rte. 7 and follow directions above.

THE BOULDERS INN
Lake Waramaug, New Preston, Connecticut

Carolyn Woollen drew another cup of delicious tea from the samovar and I helped myself to two lumps of sugar and a dollop of cream. She passed me a plate of homemade breads and cakes.

For a moment we just sat there looking out across Lake Waramaug, now comfortably covered with a good blanket of snow and basking in the brilliance of colors and hues created by the sinking sun. Blue waters, white sails, and ruddy swimmers give this same lake an altogether different look in summer.

Carolyn put her finger to her lips and then her hand to her ear, "If we listen quietly I think we can hear the Canada geese talking to each other."

There was a stamping of feet at the back door and I could hear the clatter of cross-country skis being stacked in the corner. Some red-cheeked guests came trooping across the living room and gathered around the fireplace warming their hands and exclaiming about the wonderful time they had had on the trails.

In the 1980 edition of this book I reported on the progress that Carolyn and her husband Jim and their children Peter, Mary, and Byron had made during their first full season at the inn. At that time their objective had been to provide a small intimate retreat where care, attention, and a homelike atmosphere would blend with the physical setting and facilities. Now I was ready for another update:

"Oh, we've all had a wonderful time. In addition to attending to our guests, we've extended our outdoor dining area with two terraced decks overlooking the lake. We did this in time for last summer's guests and the shady area under the pine trees proved a very popular place for dining.

"We installed fireplaces in our cottages which certainly make them very cozy. They all have either patios or balconies.

"Summer and fall are well-established here by a tradition of vacationers and by those enjoying the autumn foliage, but more and more of our guests are coming during the colder months because it's an area of such incredible beauty. I think it's quite reminiscent of the Scottish hills and it's hard to realize that New York is just eighty miles south of us. Guests can skate on the lake, toboggan on our old ski hill, and hike the mountain trails which actually start from the back door. We're only twenty minutes away from the Mohawk

Mountain ski center. For guests who are more inclined toward reading or conversaton, we have a whole corner of the living room set aside as a library."

Carolyn excused herself to serve more cups of coffee and tea, and since the sun had now completely set, the candles in the dining room were being lit and my thoughts began to turn to dinner.

I picked up the menu to see what the winter offerings would be and found veal Provencal, baked stuffed shrimp, and a fresh fish of the day. "Ragout of beef is very popular in the wintertime," Carolyn said, as she rejoined me. "And we do chicken paprikasch which is boned chicken breast in a sour cream sauce accented with sweet Hungarian paprika."

The cross-country skiers and hikers would have a hearty meal at the Boulder Inn tonight.

One brief snatch of conversation caught my ear: "You know, Emily, it's so good here right now, can you imagine what it's like in the summer!"

BOULDERS INN, Lake Waramaug, New Preston, Ct 06777; 203-868-7918. A 15-room year-round resort-inn, 20 mi. north of Danbury, 40 mi. west of Hartford. From Memorial Day to Labor Day, three meals a day served to travelers as well as guests. Monday dinner an informal meal for houseguests only. Lodging during this period either on American or mod. American plan. From September through May, breakfast is served every day; dinner, Tuesday through Saturday. Open on Thanksgiving, closed Christmas Eve and Christmas Day. Tennis, swimming, boating, sailing, fishing, antiquing, hiking on mountain trails, bicycling, xc skiing, sledding. Golf, horseback riding, and downhill skiing nearby. 20 min. from chamber music concert series July through August. Not suitable for children under 6. The Woollen Family, Innkeepers.

Directions: From I-84, take Exit 7 and follow Rte. 7 north to Rte. 202 (formerly 25) through New Milford. Proceed 8 mi. to New Preston then 1½ mi. to inn on Rte. 45.

WEST LANE INN
Ridgefield, Connecticut

Our conversation first started in the bright, cheerful breakfast room at the West Lane Inn, and continued as we carried our cups of coffee out to the broad porch to enjoy the morning sunshine. "I guess I'm what is known as a commercial traveler!" he remarked. "That's a sort of old-fashioned term." We settled down into the handsome white wicker chairs and he continued, "Actually, I'm from Yorkshire. In England, business travelers like myself stay at places similar to

this . . . converted great houses, mansions, or country houses."

He gestured with his free hand toward the broad lawn with its azaleas, tulips, roses, and maple and oak trees. "This is what I like about the place," he continued enthusiastically. "The simple garden and the quiet. The bedrooms are certainly much larger than my bedroom at home, and some have working fireplaces. I've stayed here a number of times, because I find it convenient to leave New York about four o'clock in the afternoon, avoiding the rush-hour traffic. I'm here in plenty of time to take a stroll around the village or a walk in the woods. It's up early next morning and on my way, either to Hartford or Boston, and I've had a good night's rest. Fortunately, there are telephones right in the room so I can make some business appointments or even call home.

"They have a very hospitable arrangement here with snacks in the pantry until ten p.m., in case I arrive a little late," he asserted. "And breakfast can either be continental, which is included with the price of the room, or can be larger, more like my British breakfast. They had sliced bananas or fresh berries, poached eggs on toast, and things like that.

"Oddly enough," he said, "Ridgefield was the scene of a serious battle between the British and the Americans during the Revolutionary War. One of the British cannonballs went through Keeler's Tavern and so surprised the few occupants that they ran for the woods. Another cannonball hit one of the sturdy oak cornerposts of the tavern and is still embedded there."

While we were talking, I noticed that the guests at the West Lane on this particular morning were about equally divided between businessmen, like my newfound acquaintance, and couples or families traveling with children. The latter group must have found the oversized bedrooms very convenient. The youngsters can watch the color TV.

By North American standards Ridgefield, with large, graceful trees, is a very old village, founded in 1708 by a small group of citizens from Norwalk. These early settlers laid out the town with great care, which can still be seen today. Many of the houses date from the early 19th century.

The building which later became the West Lane Inn was constructed in the early 1800s. The underlying colonial or Federalist architecture has been overshadowed by a number of Victorian features including, thankfully, the aforementioned broad porch. The main hall and reception area, with dark wood paneling, an impressive staircase, and wing chairs, creates a very quiet and relaxing mood.

Breakfast is the only regular meal served, although the staff is very happy to advise guests on the restaurants in the area.

WEST LANE INN, 22 West Lane, Ridgefield, Conn. 06877; 203-438-7323. A 14-room inn in a quiet residential village in southwest Connecticut. Approx. 1 hour from N.Y.C. Open every day in the year. Breakfast and light snacks available until 10:30 p.m. Convenient to many museums and antique shops. Golf, tennis, swimming, and xc skiing and other outdoor recreation available nearby. No pets. Maureen Mayer, Innkeeper.

Directions: From New York: follow I-684 to Exit 6, turn right on Rte. 35, 12 mi. to Ridgefield. Inn is on left. From Hartford: Exit I-84 on Rte. 7 south and follow Rte. 35 to Ridgefield.

THE HOMESTEAD INN
Greenwich, Connecticut

I drove east on 59th Street, picked up the entrance to the FDR Drive, drove north, followed the Triborough Bridge and picked up I-95 headed for Connecticut. Even with the heavier late afternoon traffic, I was outside Greenwich in about fifty minutes and turned off at Exit 3. Following my CIBR directions, I knew I would be at The Homestead Inn in time for my dinner appointment.

Almost immediately, I was in the residential area of this fashionable New York suburb, where beautiful homes were set back from the road. I turned into the parklike grounds of the inn, with its gently floodlit trees. It was quite a transformation from the hustle and bustle of the city such a short time ago!

My hostesses were the co-innkeepers, Lessie Davison and

Nancy Smith, two attractive, enthusiastic women who, a few years ago, saw the possibilities of restoring the property, and then spent a year returning it to its 19th-century effulgence.

"It's hard to realize," Lessie commented, "that the original building was built in 1799, because in 1859 it was completely remodeled in the 'Carpenter Gothic' architecture which was so popular during the Victorian era. However, there are sections of the house that have some beautiful old exposed beams and posts, and chimneys which are part of the original building."

Between the two of them, Lessie and Nancy made certain that I saw every single one of the thirteen attractive guest rooms in the inn. Each one is quite different and has a very distinctive name which usually has some connection with the décor of the room. For instance, the Butterfly Room has the butterfly wallpaper pattern; the Bride's Room has a canopied bed; and the Sleigh Bedroom has beautiful sleigh beds. There's a Quail Room, a Mary Jane Room, and even a Tassel Room. All are splendidly furnished, including many antiques, and such comforts and appurtenances as clock radios, electric blankets, two pillows for every head, lots of books and magazines, and very modern bathrooms which contain the only make-up mirrors I've ever seen at a country inn. A continental breakfast, included in the room charge, is served to overnight guests.

The restaurant at the Homestead is called "La Grange," and the French cuisine is the creation of Jacques Theibeult from Paris, whom I met briefly in a tour of the kitchen. I enjoyed a sumptuous dinner featuring a first course of Billi-bi, a bisque of mussel which is served either hot or chilled. For the main course, I chose quenelles of salmon served with champagne—delicious. The dessert was a linzer torte, although I wavered between the dark and the white chocolate mousses. The restaurant has a timbered ceiling, and the tables looked most attractive with fine linens and fresh flowers. Nancy pointed out that the menu changes with the seasons.

With dinner over, we sat for a moment in the Backgammon Room, a drawing room with green felt walls and wooden shutters. "We have quite a few honeymooners who stay with us." said Lessie, "and also people who enjoy roaming in the many antique shops in the area."

The Homestead Inn—an elegant, sophisticated inn in a suburban setting.

THE HOMESTEAD INN, 420 Field Point Rd., Greenwich, Conn. 06830; 203-869-7500. A 13-room inn located in the residential area of a suburb, 45 mins. from New York City. Lunch served Mon. thru Fri. Dinner served daily except Christmas, New Year's, Good Friday, and perhaps others. Located a short distance from Connecticut countryside and shore scenes. Accessible by train from New York City. No amusements for children under twelve. No pets. Lessie B. Davison, Nancy K. Smith, Innkeepers.

Directions: The inn is 3 min. from Rte. I-95 via Exit 3. Turn left at traffic light, immediately before the railroad underpass. Go two blocks to end of street (stop sign). Turn left, proceed ¼ mi. to inn. on right.

TOWN FARMS INN
Middletown, Connecticut

In August, 1980, the kitchen of the Town Farms Inn was totally destroyed by fire. Innkeeper Bill Winterer called me the next day, and on January 16, 1981, I drove from Stockbridge to Middletown to see first-hand the results of a record-setting reconstruction. I am repeating once again the account of my visit on January, 1981. It gives credit where credit is due:

Even though I knew that the main parts of the two buildings which go to make up the Town Farms Inn had not been damaged by fire, I breathed a sigh of relief to see the brick structures intact and glowing in the afternoon sunset.

As soon as I stepped inside the front door, manager Ray Terrill greeted me and pointed out that this elegant area with its crackling fireplace and sofas and chairs, used as a living room, was under almost a foot of water the morning after the fire. "It was necessary to redecorate the room and also to reupholster all the furniture," he said. "We had to send to France for the fabrics." I'm certain that someone visiting the inn for the first time with no foreknowledge of

the fire would never suspect such a condition ever existed. The beautiful print of early Middletown was now back on the wall, and the Staffordshire dogs grinned from their accustomed places on the mantel.

A tour of the remainder of the inn, including the three dining rooms, convinced me that everything was shipshape. The collection of photographs of early Middletown and New Haven, which adorned one whole wall of the study was back in place, and the candles in the Indian Room, with its low ceiling and prints of early Connecticut Indian chiefs, were being lighted. Two of the waitresses were just completing some of the details in the River Room which is one and a half stories high and has Palladian windows at one end. The mural of the river scene of 100 years ago, which takes up one entire wall, was undamaged, and the view of the Connecticut River and the boatyards on the opposite shore was still unobstructed. Ray said that the two handsome chandeliers were found by Bill and Vicky Winterer in Paris, but the glass was made right there in Connecticut. "They had suffered from smoke damage and I personally polished every piece," he declared somewhat ruefully.

I asked him about the party for the firemen on the previous night. "The fire chief said it was the first time in his 25 years on the force that he remembers receiving such an expression of gratitude for what he termed 'simply doing our job.'"

Bill Winterer in a subsequent conversation told me how pleased he was with the splendid job being done by Ray and executive chef Robert Cardinal. "Together," he said, "they bring to Town Farms a breadth of food knowledge unique in Connecticut."

Bob and I discussed the menu. There was fresh boneless trout seasoned with mushrooms, shallots, and capers prepared in white wine; roasted Muscovy duck sliced, dusted with grated Gruyere cheese, and glazed; small venison steaks studded with red peppercorns, sautéed and then wrapped in herbed crepes and served in brown sauce with red currant brandy; and venison, rabbit, and wild duck braised with a selection of vegetables and served in a brioche.

Town Farms is even more impressive than ever, although the fire has of necessity postponed Bill and Vicky Winterer's plans to add lodging rooms. Bill says of the firefighters: "If it hadn't been for those guys, we wouldn't be here tonight."

TOWN FARMS INN, Silver St., Middletown, Conn. 06457; 203-347-7438. A riverside restaurant just a few minutes from the center of Middletown. Lunch and dinner served daily except Christmas Eve and Christmas Day. Wesleyan Univ. nearby. Long Island Sound about 40 min. away. Bill and Vicky Winterer, Innkeepers.

Directions: From I-91 follow Rte. 9 south to Middletown and take Exit 12. Follow signs to Town Farms Inn.

GRISWOLD INN
Essex, Connecticut

How quickly time flies. I was reminded of this in a recent letter I had from Bill Winterer, the innkeeper at the Griswold Inn, who pointed out that it has been ten years since he acquired the Griswold Inn and what a wonderful experience it has been for him and his wife Vicky. For example, he wrote, "This last weekend we had our annual Halloween Party for the town children at Griswold Square" (a reproduction of a small village meeting place formed from the early 19th-century buildings across the street from the Griswold Inn).

"In addition to several hundred costumed children, along with their parents, we had the Sailing Masters of 1812, which is our fife and drum corps. They played a concert around a roaring bonfire and we served about 1,000 of our homemade sausages to the children and all of the friends and parents and neighbors. We served English beer on draft to the adults and fresh sweet cider to the youngsters. It was truly a lovely evening."

I was reminded of a similar celebration that takes place every year at Griswold Square a few days before Christmas when everybody gathers to sing Christmas carols and enjoy Christmas music by the Eastern Brass Quintet. It's a rather bittersweet memory for me because the late Governor Ella Grasso was my partner at dinner on that evening.

In the true tradition of many old inns, the "Gris" is the center of all kinds of community activity in Essex. This has been true since 1776 when the inn was first opened for business. It even survived the War of 1812 when the British marines destroyed the Essex fleet by fire and commandeered and occupied the inn during their brief Connecticut Valley campaign.

Today, the Griswold Inn has within its many dining rooms and parlors a remarkable collection of marine paintings, prints, ship models, firearms, binnacles, ship's clocks, a pot-bellied stove, humorous posters and prints, a genuine popcorn machine, and much more.

It also has a dining room constructed from an abandoned New Hampshire covered bridge, and still another dining room where a wall rocks to and fro creating the impression of being on shipboard.

There are 22 guest rooms, all of which now have private baths. One, the Oliver Cromwell Suite, is named after the first warship of the Revolutionary navy which was built in Essex, a shipbuilding center during the Revolution. Today, the town is the center of yacht-building activity and it's possible to watch the beautiful ships being constructed.

The menu is basically American with a wide selection of fresh and salt-water fish, also beef and lamb dishes which have been popular in this country from the very beginning. A Hunt Breakfast is served every Sunday with great long tables of fried chicken, herring, lamb, kidneys, eggs, grits (honest), creamed chipped beef, and the inn's sausage.

Bill's letter continued, "We're completely recovered from the fire at the Town Farms Inn and I'm anxious to show you the Dock n'

Dine fishhouse at Saybrook Point. It is on the nearly five acres, sitting directly at the mouth of the Connecticut River. Diners can look across Long Island Sound and view ships coming in from the sea. I believe we're going to change the name in the future to Saybrook Point."

And so, indeed, time does move on and while there always seems to be progress of some sort at the "Gris," nevertheless many things remain unchanged. On foggy nights when one can almost hear the diaphone of the Old Saybrook lighthouse, it's easy to feel transported back to another century, and indeed Essex and the inn have themselves been spectators to many stirring events of the past.

GRISWOLD INN, Main St., Essex, Conn. 06426; 203-767-0991. A 22-room inn in a waterside town, steps away from the Connecticut River, and located near the Eugene O'Neill Theatre, Goodspeed Opera House, Ivoryton Playhouse, Gillette Castle, Mystic Village, Valley Railroad and Hammonasset State Beach. European plan. Complimentary continental breakfast served daily to inn guests. Lunch and dinner served daily to travelers. Hunt breakfast served Sundays. Closed Christmas Eve and Christmas Day. Day sailing on inn's 44-foot ketch by appointment. Bicycles, tennis, and boating nearby. Victoria and William G. Winterer, Innkeepers.

Directions: From I-95 take Exit 69 and travel north on Rte. 9 to Exit 3, Essex. Turn right at stoplight and follow West Ave. to center of town. Turn right onto Main St. and proceed down to water and inn.

MOUNTAIN VIEW INN
Norfolk, Connecticut

It was just the kind of night to be playing Monopoly on the living room floor in front of a crackling fire, and that's exactly what was going on at the Mountain View Inn. There were four guests dressed in cross-country ski clothing with a ruddy glow that meant an afternoon on some of the nearby trails. They gave me a warm "hiya" as I passed through on the way to a second-floor bedroom.

I had made it a point to arrive well before dinner so that I could have a short chat with Pamela and Josef Quirinale, who came to innkeeping about two years ago from a background in the theater. Pamela was an actress and Josef was a production coordinator.

Even in the fading light of late afternoon I could see that they had redecorated the exterior of this stately Victorian country home in an authentic Victorian color scheme of cream with coffee brown and dark brown trim. It was a dramatic treatment.

Later, as I chatted with Pamela and Josef about their show business background, I asked how running an inn is like putting on

a show, and Pamela replied, "We feel that it's very much the same as operating on a basic theater schedule. Monday night we're dark and Tuesday and Wednesday we're in rehearsal. Thursday is preview night, and then Friday, Saturday, and Sunday the show is on — Sunday afternoon is the finale. The atmosphere and the decor are all part of the drama. There's drama in putting on a meal, too — even the way Josef arranges the food on the plate."

The conversation led naturally to a discussion of their menu, and Josef who doubles as chef explained some of their rather unique ideas about the cuisine. "We usually have about two seafoods, a steak or filet, veal, and chicken or pasta. We change the menu about twice a month and keep it to five or six entrées. We try to do the more unusual dishes. Sometimes we take something from a different country to make it a little more exciting. For example, during the summer we have international buffets on Friday nights before the Yale Summer School concerts, and a different national cuisine is featured each week; not ordinary, but something extra special. Pamela loves to decorate especially for those occasions."

Along with Sadie, the golden retriever, and Baby Nugget, the orange cat, Pamela took me on a tour of the country inn-style bedrooms on the second and third floor where there was an interesting assortment of furniture including iron beds, antique backboards and patchwork quilts. Much of it looked like somebody's family heirlooms. One bathroom had a chaise lounge.

At dinner Pamela placed me in a corner table next to the fireplace in the dining room. After a few minutes the Monopoly players came in and soon the dining room was buzzing with hearty appetites and lively conversation.

Norfolk is a village of gentle persuasions in the Litchfield hills of northwest Connecticut and has for many years been the scene of the Yale Summer School concerts considered by many to be on a par with those of nearby Tanglewood and Saratoga. On a snowy winter day with the lovely old church and the triangular-shaped village green accented by the falling snow, it was the personification of Old New England.

The Mountain View Inn is show business's loss and country innkeeping's gain.

MOUNTAIN VIEW INN, Rte. 272, Norfolk, Connecticut 06058; 203-542-5595. An 8-room village inn with a summer cottage in northwest Connecticut near many historic, cultural, and recreational points of interest including the Yale Summer School of Music concerts. Modified American plan only on weekends. European plan on other days. Breakfast included in price of room. Open for dinner Fri., Sat., Sun. year-round, and also on Thurs. during summer and fall. Dinner reservations for Mon.-Wed. require 1-wk. advance reservation. Closed Christmas Eve and Christmas Day. Golf, tennis, swimming, hiking, mountain climbing, bicycles, Alpine and xc skiing nearby. Pamela and Josef Quirinale, Innkeepers.

Directions: Norfolk is on U.S. 44 which runs east-west. North-south roads which intersect 44 include U.S. 7, I-91, and U.S. 22. The Mountain View is located on Rte. 44, ¼ mi. on 272 south.

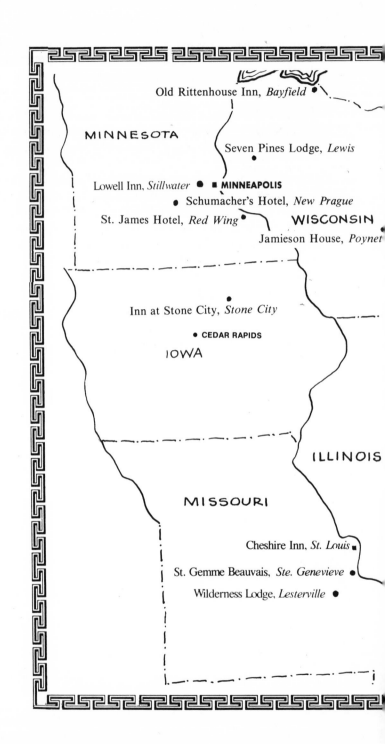

Stafford's Bay View Inn, *Petoskey*

White Gull Inn, *Fish Creek*

MICHIGAN

Michillinda Beach Lodge, *Whitehall*

DETROIT

Botsford Inn, *Farmington*

National House, *Marshall*

CLEVELAND

The Patchwork Quilt, *Middlebury*

Welshfield Inn, *Burton*

OHIO

COLUMBUS ■ ● Buxton Inn, *Granville*

· INDIANAPOLIS

INDIANA

Golden Lamb, *Lebanon*

CINCINNATI

EVANSVILLE

Midwest
Central Time Zone

Ohio

THE GOLDEN LAMB
Lebanon, Ohio

An antique music box tinkled merrily in the lobby of the Golden Lamb and on the table a handsome bowl was filled with punch. Decorative blue wooden interior shutters, a glowing fire in the fireplace, an old Shaker stove, flooring of intricate tile, and antique chairs and benches completed the picture.

The inn has played host to distinguished visitors from many lands, as well as many American presidents and notables. In fact, its history dates back more than 170 years.

Speaking of presidents, on this particular evening a little poster in the lobby described the favorite meal of Martin Van Buren when he stayed at the Golden Lamb.

Since this lovely old inn is a part of the heartland of America, it stands to reason that the main dishes would be representative of American cooking. For example, there is filet mignon, rainbow trout, and fried Kentucky ham steak. Other dishes offered that we think of as typically American are roast duckling with wild rice dressing, flounder, Warren County turkey, and pork tenderloin. When possible, vegetables from the Ohio countryside are used.

Rooms at the Golden Lamb would enhance a museum of early Americana. There are huge four-posters, intricately carved chests and tables, and an almost priceless collection of 19th-century prints. The rooms are named for the distinguished visitors of the past including Dickens, DeWitt Clinton, and Ulysses S. Grant.

On this visit I occupied a twin-bedded room named for Samuel Clemens. It had an old-fashioned school desk, twin maple beds, a handsome blanket chest, and a rocking chair with a rush seat. On the top floor there are antique rooms for guests' observation. Among them are a Shaker pantry with a complete description of all the kitchen items — extra chairs hang from pegs.

There is also a Shaker Retiring Room where the bed has a trundle bed beneath it. There are examples of Shaker costume hanging from pegs, and quite a few of the simple cabinets, desks, and stoves. Innkeeper Jack Reynolds commented on the relationship between the Ohio Shakers and the New Lebanon, New York, Shakers who lived just over the mountain from the Berkshires, and he suggested that I visit the Shaker Room at the Warren County Museum just a few doors away. He also mentioned the reproduction of a 19th-century village green surrounded by tiny shops and stores. "It's all in the museum," he explained.

This section of Ohio has really become quite a holiday and vacation focal point. There's the Little Miami, Ohio's scenic river with fishing, canoeing, hiking, and riding. The Glendower State Museum is a restored Greek Revival mansion; and one of the most popular places is King's Island, centered around a 33-story replica of the Eiffel Tower, where there is a variety of rides and entertainment, as well as a Jack Nicklaus golf center.

While her husband was signing the register, I heard a lady who was visiting the Golden Lamb remark, "It's like a 19th-century sampler."

THE GOLDEN LAMB INN, 27 S. Broadway, Lebanon, Ohio 45036; 513-932-5065. A historic 20-room village inn in the heart of Ohio farming country on U.S. Hwys. 63, 42, and 48. European plan. 19 rooms with private baths. Breakfast served only on Sundays. Lunch and dinner served daily except Christmas. Golf and tennis nearby. No pets. Jackson Reynolds, Innkeeper.

Directions: From I-71, exit Rte. 48 N, 3 mi. west to Lebanon. From I-75, exit Rte. 63 E, 7 mi. east to Lebanon.

THE BUXTON INN
Granville, Ohio

It was the Saturday afternoon of the Big Game in Granville; Denison U. was playing Ohio State. The weather was fantastic — the temperature was just right and the beautiful trees of Granville could not have been more cooperative with their bright yellows, dusty russets, faded greens, and all the shades in between.

Granville is a most attractive and appealing town with its beautiful homes, broad streets, spacious lawns, and a wonderful feeling of warmth and openness that always gives me a lift. It was in 1974 that I first visited Granville and the Buxton Inn and met

innkeepers Orville and Audrey Orr and their daughters Melanie and Amy.

On this September afternoon, the inn was positively dazzling in a new coat of salmon-orange-pink, which provided a colorful background for the white window trim and railings, and the black shutters.

The Buxton was originally built in 1812, and the Orr family has recreated the atmosphere of a country inn of that period, even to the point of having waitresses, hosts, and hostesses dressed in carefully researched costumes of the time.

From the day of my first visit I have been noting with great pleasure and pride the progress made by the inn and all of the innkeepers. For example, Melanie Orr, who is now 18 and working in the kitchen as a cook, is able to prepare every item on the menu. Her interest in all kinds of outdoor sports continues.

Amy, the younger, who was my first guide in Granville, will be finishing her sophmore year in high school and is on the cheerleading squad. She joined me for a few moments after having her horseback riding lesson. She's quite the young lady now.

Audrey and Orville have been very much involved with maintaining the Buxton's reputation for excellent food and service, and also in expanding some of the features of the property. For example, at the rear of the inn an elegant gazebo has been built and is surrounded by a small pond.

The inn gift shop also seems to have grown since my last visit and has, among other things, an unusual collection of china kittens and cats in various poses. This is because one of the most famous personalities at the inn is Major Buxton, a beautiful, tawny tiger cat, named for a 19th-century owner of the inn who operated it for forty years.

At the moment, there are three bedrooms for guests at this inn, although Orville said that he had a number of ideas for further accommodations in the future.

There are several different dining rooms. One of them has low ceilings and the posts and beams are painted with colors that are similar to the exterior hues. I noted the attractive pewter underplates and handsome candlesticks. A new dining room called the Wine Cellar has a cozy feeling with Tiffany-type lamps and decorative wine bottles. The inn also has a modest outdoor dining area which is used for lunch and dinner during the clement months.

The Buxton has one of the most extensive menus that I have ever encountered with several novel and original dishes, I've always enjoyed the grilled ham steak with Cumberland sauce and the roast duckling with orange-cranberry sauce.

It was great to be back in Granville and just to top the day off, if I remember correctly, Denison won the game.

THE BUXTON INN, 313 E. Broadway, Granville, Ohio 43023; 614-587-0001. A 3-room inn in a college town in central Ohio near Denison University, the Indian Mounds Museum and the Heisey Glass Museum. European plan. Lunch and dinner served daily. Closed Christmas Day. Golf, tennis, horseback riding, cultural activities nearby. No pets. Orville and Audrey Orr, Innkeepers.

Directions: Take Granville exit from I-70. Travel north 8 mi. on Rte. 37 into Granville.

WELSHFIELD INN
Burton, Ohio

I was standing in the kitchen at the Welshfield Inn talking with owner-chef Brian Holmes about two things very near to his heart. One was the preparation of baked and mashed potatoes, and the other was his philosophy of keeping a restaurant. The planned additions to the kitchen, which were on the drawing board during my last visit, had now become a reality and everything was moving with great efficiency.

"Norman, when I bake potatoes I believe in having the skin clean enough to eat; I like to eat the skin myself, especially because it contains so many minerals. First we scrub the potatoes thoroughly and put shortening or oil on them. We put them in the oven at about 400° to 425° and after they've been in the oven for an hour and a quarter they should be ready—I test the doneness by inserting a fine-tine fork.

"We're known far and wide for our whipped Idaho potatoes. We whip them in an electric mixer which puts more air into them and makes them much whiter. These are also made in small batches so

they're fresh. One of the secrets of good food is preparing in small quantities. I learned that from an old-time restaurant man."

A raisin sauce for the baked ham was bubbling on the stove and the wonderful aroma of apple pies already in the oven filled the kitchen. There were pans with baked acorn squash, stuffed zucchini, and the makings of fresh strawberry shortcake. "Our recipe for Indian pudding came from Cape Cod," Brian said. "We took it as a compliment when one of our customers said it tasted exactly like the pudding at the Red Inn at Provincetown."

One of the waitresses dressed in an attractive early American costume complete with a white duster cap carried a tray of fresh rolls into the dining room. "That's another thing," he said, "we never use mixes—our rolls and breads are made from scratch."

We took a few minutes to walk through the many dining rooms and I even stopped to drop a coin in the famous nickelodeon. "I hope you've had a chance to visit our Country Store," he said. "It's expanding all the time and Polly is very much involved with that."

The Welshfield Inn is a country restaurant about 30 miles from Cleveland and is extremely well-known in the area as "the" place to go for Easter, Mother's Day, Thanksgiving, and Christmas. On the day of my visit a great number of families were dining at tables of eight and ten.

Brian paused long enough at the front door to bid me goodbye and he had a final thought for me:

"I'm known for being fussy and particular," he said. "I believe if you're in the restaurant business, the main thing in that business is *food*. Food preparation and serving of food is most important and Polly and I feel that nothing is too good for our customers. I'm happy to say that we seem to be able to please more people every year and a great many of them arrive with your book tucked underneath their arms. You've extended your territory since your first visit in 1972 and we're even more pleased than ever to be included."

Brian, it is *we* who are proud to have you.

WELSHFIELD INN, Rte. 422, Burton, Ohio 44021; 216-834-4164. A country restaurant on Rte. 422, 28 mi. east of Cleveland. No lodgings. Lunch and dinner served weekdays. Dinner only served on Sundays and holidays. Closed the week of July 4th and three weeks after Jan. 1. Closed Mondays except Labor Day. Near Sea World and Holden Arboretum. Brian and Polly Holmes, Innkeepers.

Directions: On U.S. 422 at intersection of Ohio 700, midway between Cleveland and Youngstown, Ohio.

WHAT IS INNKEEPING REALLY LIKE?

"Sunday, our dog barked (while standing on our couch staring out the window) and I said my usual 'shut up.' This was at 7:30 a.m. I did look out the window, however, and without my glasses saw what appeared to be a horse walking our paths. With benefit of glasses, I saw a moose! I called Doris, Ted, and hunted down Fred in the dining room and everyone watched as the moose walked to the water, using only the well-groomed paths, back, across the gully on our land and into the adjoining field. You know we are not in a remote location, so seeing a moose did blow my mind the entire day (kept thinking of those weird TV ads where bulls walk into restaurants, etc.). It was a healthy animal so the game warden didn't bother to come out." — Maine

"We are finding the nicest thing about innkeeping is having repeat guests come back. It's like having family or old friends rejoin us — but better yet they pay and don't stay too long! We have made some fast friendships and feel that we certainly made the right decision to become innkeepers. So often we have said that we don't know of any other business we could have undertaken that would have returned to us so many rewards." — Maine

Continued on page 215

Missouri

ST. GEMME BEAUVAIS
Ste. Genevieve, Missouri

I was on Interstate 55 coming south from St. Louis after a most pleasant visit at the Cheshire Inn. In a few minutes I would be turning off onto Highway 32 and paying another visit to the town of Ste. Genevieve. In 1974 I visited this historic Missouri community for the first time and met Frankye and Boats Donze and enjoyed staying in their little inn, St. Gemme Beauvais. At that time I also had a tour of the old part of the town and visited many of the carefully restored houses including the Amoureaux House and the Beauvais House, both of which are the personal projects of the Donzes.

I turned down the village street and soon found myself in front of the red brick inn with its two-story white pillars. As I approached, Frankye opened the door and said, "I'm so glad that you could come again." Boats joined us, we had a pleasant reunion, and they told me all the news.

They were very enthusiastic about the number of people who have visited the inn from reading about it in *CIBR*. "There are people from all over the country and our telephone is ringing constantly," exclaimed Frankye. "Travelers with "the book" just seem to love the inn and the town and I have taken quite a few of them on a tour. Sometimes we are terribly busy. A lot of people who saw the picture of you and the articles in the St. Louis papers have been here. Jim Prentice from the Cheshire Inn, also recommends us to his guests."

I looked around the dining room where we were having a cup of tea. Of course, nothing has really changed. Why should it? The beautiful walnut ladderback chairs, the Belgian lace curtains, the marble fireplace, the fine china, and the graceful stemware had the elegant look of a century ago. Because they were anxious to preserve the heritage of the town, Frankye said that they put great emphasis on French dishes for both breakfast and lunch. "We have crêpes, French mushroom omelettes, quiche Lorraine, French toast with ginger fruit sauce, and other specialties," she explained.

The bedrooms are done in what I call "19th-century Missouri" which means that they have a collection of many different kinds of Victorian antiques including marble top bureaus, high-back beds, and old-fashioned flowered wallpaper. Incidentally, there are eight different suites in the inn, and each has at least two rooms. In a few instances there are two double beds. The bridal suite has an elegant crystal chandelier and big windows overlooking the main street.

During my earlier visit, I had only visited a few of the old, restored buildings, so I asked Frankye to show me more of historic Ste. Genevieve that afternoon. Any home built after 1860 is considered modern.

It was great fun to see the Donzes again. They are two of the most sincerely involved innkeepers that I have ever met. Just before leaving, I spotted once again the little sign that expresses the philosophy of this homey inn: "There are no strangers here, just friends we haven't met."

ST. GEMME BEAUVAIS, 78 N. Main St., Ste. Genevieve, Mo. 63670; 314-883-5744. An 8-room village inn about 1½ hrs. from St. Louis. Modified American plan includes breakfast only. Breakfast served daily. Lunch served Mon. thru Sat. Open year-round. Closed Thanksgiving and Christmas Day. Golf, hunting, and fishing nearby. No pets. Frankye and Boats Donze, Innkeepers.

Directions: From St. Louis, south on I-55 to Hwy. 32. Exit east on 32 to Hwy. 61 to the Ste. Genevieve exit.

CHESHIRE INN AND LODGE
St. Louis, Missouri

Although the Cheshire Inn is hardly a small inn in the country, it is as British as anything one might find this side of London's Piccadilly Circus. Imagine finding four red double-deck London buses and a Tudor-style building with half timbers just a few miles from the Mississippi River!

For the most part, furnishings and decorations in both the Inn and the Lodge are the result of a passion for collecting shared by proprietors Steve and Barbara Apted, and this passion extends to the lodging rooms, some of which are named for prominent English literary figures such as Johnson, Galsworthy, Dickens, and Tennyson.

I stayed in the Richard the Lionhearted Room in the Lodge which had a canopied bed with curtains around it, reminding me of

several country house hotels in Britain. When the sun came up, the matching rich red curtains at the windows created a marvelous red glow. The television set was hidden in an old oak chest.

Houseguests enjoy a breakfast buffet which offers an endless array of eggs (poached, scrambled, fried, soft boiled and hard boiled), bacon, and several different kinds of fresh breads, and delicious hot chocolate.

The first page of the very extensive dinner menu explains why the Cheshire Inn has been created in an English atmosphere. It says in part: "Times were hard in 'Merrie Olde England.' People worked hard for long hours and to compensate, learned how to live and live well on the simple pleasures of everyday life. At sundown they would repair to their hearthsides for a warming bowl of soup followed by rich roast beef.

"At Cheshire we try to recreate this jolly period with costumes, recipes from old books, music, and a general air of 'hail stranger, hail friend, sit down and rest yourself, partake of what we offer!'"

The descriptions of the main courses are enough to give one the appetite of Henry VIII. One of the specialties of the house is roast prime rib of beef served with Yorkshire pudding and horseradish sauce. The meat is roasted on a slowly turning spit to keep in the natural juices and flavor.

Another specialty is roast duck which, according to the menu, is prepared, "in the manner preferred by Charles Dickens." The individual beef Wellington is a succulent tenderloin of beef topped with paté and encased in flaky pastry, served with Bordelaise sauce. There are many, many more selections on the menu including, veal Marsala, shrimp Tempura, Coq Au Vin, Alaskan King crab legs, several combinations of prime rib and seafood, and many types of steaks. The most popular dessert is the English trifle; or perhaps it is the Missouri apple pie served warm with cheese or ice cream; or maybe it's both.

I enjoy staying at the Cheshire Inn and Lodge when visiting St. Louis because it's right across the street from the park where there's so much happening in both summer and winter. There are plans to have horse and carriage rides available for guests' pleasure.

CHESHIRE INN and LODGE, 6300 Clayton Rd., St. Louis, Mo. 63117; 314-647-7300. A 110-room English-style inn, 1 block off Hwy. 40 near Forest Park. European plan only. Breakfast, lunch, and dinner served to travelers daily. Accommodations available every day of the year. Restaurant closed on New Year's Day, Memorial Day, July 4th, Labor Day, and Christmas Day. Pool, bicycles on grounds. Boating, golf, tennis, carriage rides, and riding nearby. St. Louis Art Museum, zoo, Gateway Arch, and opera nearby. Jim Prentice, Innkeeper.

Directions: Just off Hwy. 40 at Clayton Rd. and Skinker Blvd. on southwest corner of Forest Park. From the east, take Clayton Rd. exit. From the west, take McCausland Ave. exit, north two blocks to Clayton Rd.

I do not include lodging rates in the descriptions, for the very nature of an inn means that there are lodgings of various sizes, with and without baths, in and out of season, and with plain and fancy decoration. Travelers should call ahead and inquire about the availability and rates of the many different types of rooms.

"European Plan" means that rates for rooms and meals are separate. "American Plan" means that meals are included in the cost of the room. "Modified American Plan" means that breakfast and dinner are included in the cost of the room. The rates at some inns include a continental breakfast with the lodging.

Iowa

THE INN AT STONE CITY
Anamosa, Iowa

I was luxuriating in the Jacuzzi bath at the Inn at Stone City. This in itself is paradoxical, because so much of this inn and in fact all of Stone City is really associated with the late 19th and early 20th century. The Jacuzzi, in a room with heavy stone walls, wooden furniture, and a woodburning stove, seemed somewhat out of time. Stone City is a small village twenty miles from Cedar Rapids.

It was late afternoon in early October—a golden day which would have delighted Grant Wood and the other Iowa artists in his group of fifty years ago. The colors were vivid, the sun was golden, and there was a feel of autumn in the air, although the temperature was warm.

This is Grant Wood country. In fact, perhaps the second best-known of Mr. Wood's paintings is entitled *Stone City,* painted right here in 1930. His most famous is of course, *American Gothic.*

However, long before Grant Wood established an art colony here, the village acquired a name and nature which has endured since the late 19th century. It was a community of nearly 1,000 people, most of whom worked in the stone quarries.

All of this was explained to me by innkeeper Michael Richards. He and his wife Lynette and sons Michael, fifteen and Benjamin, twelve, have not only been establishing the Inn at Stone City, but also have been very active in preserving the 19th-century buildings and *esprit.*

"Many kinds of people come here," explained Lynette, "our

guests are an integral part of the experience. Ideas are born and shared here. This is never static, never quite the same, but always an important part of the guest's stay and our way of life. We operate on a small scale so it's easy for everyone to become friends.

"Many of our visitors comment on the healing atmosphere of the valley, the inn, and the good companionship. Meals are served family style. We also provide a very appropriate setting for small-group learning events. Every year various seminars are scheduled on such topics as creativity, photography, wildlife painting, and so forth."

Michael and Lynette have the ability to involve other members of the community in the activities of the inn. I discovered that one of their best friends was actually waiting on the table, although she sat down and joined in dinner with the rest of us.

Stone City is an expanding concept. For instance, on the second weekend in June the Grant Wood Art Festival is held, attracting upwards of a hundred of the best regional artists and artisans—ten thousand people take part. In the spring and fall there are music festivals held in conjunction with the music and art department of nearby Cornell College.

"We now have a stone sculptor who has moved his studio here, as well as a metal worker and stone sculptor who came from New Mexico. One of the most noted hand-crafted gunsmiths in the country has moved his home and shop from Utah, and a limited edition press with a paper mill and a fine crafted book bindery is developing in Stone City," Michael wrote in a recent letter.

Grant Wood . . . stone quarries . . . great, well-preserved stone buildings . . . art festivals . . . folk music concerts . . . a gathering of writers, artists, and special people who want a secluded place in which to recharge their creative batteries . . . these go to make up the experience at the Inn at Stone City. It's the heart of America.

THE INN AT STONE CITY, Anamosa, Iowa 52205; 319-462-4733. A 6-room inn (no private baths) in a naturally attractive, scenic area 20 mi. from Cedar Rapids. This inn is in the historic district of the famed Grant Wood Art Colony of the 1930s. Breakfast, lunch, and dinner served by reservation to outside groups. Open Feb. 1 to Dec. 24. Volleyball, croquet, horseback riding on grounds. Golf, tennis, swimming, cross-country skiing, canoeing, backroading, hill and dale walking nearby. No credit cards. Michael and Lynette Richards, Innkeepers.

Directions: From I-80 exit north on Highway 1. Drive 25 mi. north to Anamosa. Go west on Main Street out of town on the "Ridge Road," 3 mi. to Stone City.

Michigan

THE NATIONAL HOUSE INN
Marshall, Michigan

Norman Kinney, the innkeeper at the National House Inn, was helping me to assimilate the experience of this unusual town. "Mr. Brooks was the most important factor," he said. "He was the man who had the vision of Marshall. But everybody in town has joined in. We are proud of the homes and the museums and we all work together. I am sure that we could not have restored the National House if it hadn't been a community effort. People helped out in so many ways.

"This is probably the oldest remaining hotel building in Michigan," he pointed out. "We learned that it was open in 1835 and undoubtedly was the first brick building of any kind in our county.

"At one time it was a windmill and wagon factory, and more recently an apartment building," Norman continued. "My good friend, Hal Minick and I, along with his wife Jacqueline and my wife Kathryn, decided to restore the building and return it to its original purpose.

"It has really been hard work, but underneath the dirt and grime of dozens of years, we found the solid, beautiful structure of the original brick as well as the irreplaceable woodwork. We converted the apartments into sixteen bedrooms and baths.

"As you can see, Marshall is very much a Victorian restoration. We searched everywhere—culled all the antique shops and removed furniture from our own homes. Many of our friends contributed some of their beloved pieces in order to help us recreate the atmosphere of Marshall before the turn of the century."

One of the most striking features of the National House is the passionate attention to detail. For example, each bedroom has its own ambience and there are colorful comforters, old trunks, marble top tables, bureaus, dried flower arrangements, electric lamps that are reproductions of gas lamps, candle sconces with reflectors, little corner sofas, special care with door knobs, and special attention is given to the linens. The bedroom windows overlook either the residential part of town, or a beautiful fountain in the town center park.

Breakfast is the only meal served, and is offered every morning in the dining room which has a most fetching collection of chairs and tables from great-grandfather's day. The color tones are warm brown and beige. The breakfast offerings include homebaked coffee cakes and muffins, nut breads, and the like. I spent an hour and a half at breakfast talking with many different people.

In the years since I have been visiting Marshall, which contains the finest examples of 19th-century architecture in the Midwest, a great many of the buildings and homes of the town have been added to the State of Michigan Historic Sites and to the National Register. The Marshall Historical Society sponsors a historic home tour during September of every year, certainly the most exciting yearly event in the town. However, the tour of the town, which includes at least forty historic and beautiful buildings, can be experienced at any time.

One of the most impressive of these buildings is the National House Inn.

THE NATIONAL HOUSE INN, 102 South Parkview, Marshall, Mi. 49068; 616-781-7374. An elegantly restored 16-room Victorian-period village inn. Marshall is the finest example of 19th-century architecture in the Midwest. It has 15 State Historic Sites and 6 National Register Sites. European plan includes continental breakfast. No other meals served. Open year-round. Closed Christmas Eve and Christmas Day. Tennis, golf, swimming, boating, xc skiing nearby. Norman D. Kinney, Steve Poole, Innkeepers.

Directions: From I-69 exit at Michigan Ave. in Marshall and go straight 1½ mi. to inn. From I-94 use exit 110, follow old 27 south 1½ mi. to inn.

BOTSFORD INN
Farmington Hills, Michigan

It was a late, lovely summer afternoon in Farmington and after taking one of the crossing roads from the Detroit Airport, I was on Grand Avenue headed toward Farmington and turned into the

parking lot of the Botsford Inn to see a number of people enjoying the tennis courts. A welcome breeze had come up, breaking the hot weather in Detroit, but I was still glad to know that my room at the Botsford would have air conditioning if I needed it.

I go back with the Botsford Inn—not way back to 1836 when it was first built or when the famous Innkeeper Botsford had it—but for quite a few of the more recent years. I can remember when I first heard of it, my reaction was, "Who would expect to find a country inn in Detroit." Well, the Botsford Inn isn't exactly a New England country inn, however, some of the 19th-century atmosphere has been preserved; first in the 1930s, with the help of Henry Ford, and continued by the present owner and innkeeper, John Anhut, who has a penchant for country inns.

"The late Henry Ford became interested in the preservation of the inn in 1924," John informed me. "He placed a great many of his own 19th-century antiques and treasures in it. Among them are furnishings from his country home, including a beautiful little inlaid spinet, a handsome horsehair sofa, his music boxes, a Simon Willard clock, an exquisitely inlaid mahogany table, and an attractive oil painting of the Botsford Inn showing people in the costumes of the late 19th century."

This historic inn, the oldest in Michigan, is still providing food and lodging. In 1841 it was converted into a tavern, and was a stagecoach stop on the Grand River plank road which followed the Indian trail that went to Lake Michigan. Milton C. Botsford acquired the inn in 1860 and it became a popular meeting place for drovers, farmers, and travelers.

John joined me for dinner in the main dining room with its oaken beams and broad picture window. We talked for a moment about the menu at the Botsford Inn and he had this to say, "We believe in serving predominantly American food; we aren't a French restaurant and have never tried to be one. Consequently, we have a lot of things on the menu that people come to associate with country living here in the Midwest." This idea of country food was certainly reflected in the salad bowl of crisp lettuce, pea beans, a sprinkling of carrots and celery and tomato sections. The dressing reminded me of my grandmother's, back in central New York State, a little on the vinegary side with bits of bacon in it. The short ribs that night were delicious. Each came in its own casserole and the sauce was excellent. I poured it over both the meat and potatoes; it was exactly what I wanted.

In 1836, Farmington was a day's journey from the banks of the river where Detroit was a burgeoning city. Today it is just a short drive from the hustle and bustle of the Motor City. At the Botsford Inn, everything possible has been preserved, particularly in the main building where there are many reminders of other times in Michigan.

Many of the bedrooms, furnished with reproductions, have the conveniences that American travelers often find not only helpful but necessary. Best of all, the spirit of country innkeeping and community service is very much alive.

BOTSFORD INN, 28000 Grand River Avenue, Farmington Hills, Mich. 40824; 313-474-4800. A 62-room village inn on the city line of Detroit. European plan. Dinner served daily except Monday. Breakfast and lunch Tuesday thru Saturday. Sunday brunch. Closed Christmas and New Year's Day. Tennis on grounds. Greenfield Village, skiing, and state parks nearby. John Anhut, Innkeeper.

Directions: Located in Farmington Hills on I-96 which is easily accessible from major highways in Michigan.

MICHILLINDA BEACH LODGE
Whitehall, Michigan

Whatever else there may be at Michillinda, the most exciting, pervasive, and inspiring feature is the presence of Lake Michigan. Everything at this American plan resort-inn centers around the lake and its thrilling moods. Throughout my visit with Don and Sue Eilers and their really attractive children, Kristin, eleven, and Kent, six, my attention was never far from the sound and the sight of this gorgeous body of water.

The scope of a Michillinda vacation with all of the recreational activities, both on the grounds and in the nearby town and country-side, is succinctly woven together in a very colorful brochure where the photographs show happy sun-tanned holiday-seekers of all ages

sitting in the sun overlooking the lake, walking through the unusually expansive flower gardens, playing tennis, swimming in the pool, playing miniature golf or tetherball, riding the tandem bicycle among the chalets at lakeside, or relaxing in the pine-paneled library and living room. I have seven pages of typewritten notes about my visit.

Don and Sue are ideal people to be involved in a family-oriented resort-inn. They are young and enthusiastic and have growing children of their own. As Don says, "Basically we don't run organized activities, we have all of the recreation any young person could enjoy, and yet we don't have a social director encouraging guests to 'sign-up' for this or that, and putting them into a series of time slots. We have enough grounds here and enough indoor recreation at the Surfside building so that kids can have their own fun and their parents don't have to worry about them."

Sue joined in, "I think we've always had an ideal mix of senior citizens and young children. Many of the older people don't see children as much anymore and they become 'vacation grandparents.'"

It takes a good-sized staff to keep all of the activities at Michillinda under control. Don and Sue told me that among other things they hire young people who have some theatrical and musical talent, because the staff puts on a variety show every Friday night. Sometimes the show will include a number or two by some of the guests.

Accommodations are in lakeview bedrooms with resort-furniture in both the main house and a series of small cottages and chalets on the grounds.